LIFE 1

SIMPLIFIED

WHAT YOU NEED TO KNOW
(AND WHY YOU DIDN'T)

B. Richard Bodwell

and Gregory B. Bodwell, Ph.D., J.D.

B. R. BODWELL AGENCY

CHAGRIN FALLS, OHIO

Life Insurance Simplified:
What You Need to Know (and Why You Didn't)

By B. Richard Bodwell and Gregory B. Bodwell, Ph.D., J.D.
Copyright © 2017 by B. Richard Bodwell and Gregory B. Bodwell

B. R. Bodwell Agency
41 North Main Street, #302
Chagrin Falls, Ohio 44022 USA
Tel. 1-440-247-3080
dick@brbodwellagency.com

Library of Congress Control Number: 2017905666

This book is for informational purposes only and is not financial, tax or legal advice. Seek the assistance of licensed professionals for your individual financial planning needs.

10 9 8 7 6 5 4 3 2 1

In loving memory of Frieda "Pudge" Bodwell, wife and mother

And for all who have spent their life savings

on the wrong life insurance

CONTENTS

Life Insurance Simplified:

What You Need to Know (and Why You Didn't)

Introduction

As an old song warned, "There's no one with endurance like the man who sells insurance." That certainly applies to Dick Bodwell, who has been selling life insurance for over fifty years. In that time, he has worked with thousands of clients and analyzed tens of thousands of insurance policies. He is the advisor to numerous financial planners, law and accounting firms and sports management organizations and has provided expert testimony in numerous insurance-related legal cases. He has long been aware that virtually **everyone** who buys life insurance pays too much. The industry has resisted informing people how life insurance really works. Insurance companies do give their sales agents an overview of the uses of life insurance but avoid training them thoroughly on the financial workings of insurance policies. There is a resulting widespread misconception that life insurance products are too complicated for most people to understand and are essentially all alike. Most consumers rely on the thin hope of getting a fair deal if they buy insurance from someone they know or from a big-name company, without attempting to penetrate the finer details of the agreement themselves. Of course, some of the more principled and knowledgeable agents do sincerely endeavor to offer their clients the best products available at the lowest possible cost. Unfortunately, such agents are all too rare. Too often, greed eclipses the dedication to service. Insurance companies typically pay agents the highest commissions for selling the worst products, thus discouraging sale of better, more cost-effective policies. The insurance companies as well as their agents receive more meager revenue returns from policies better serving the consumer. This reality creates a selfish motivation for those in the insurance industry to enrich themselves essentially at the expense of the public.

Dick's Realization

My personal story begins in Houston, Texas. I had been in the insurance business for seven years, trained and adept at convincing people of their need for insurance and helping them select a product to satisfy it. One afternoon, at the finale of a typical sales presentation to a local business owner, I offered my standard recommendation that my prospect purchase a "whole life" policy, one that would guarantee coverage for his "whole life," regardless of changes in his health or age. Surprisingly, while the potential customer acknowledged his need for life insurance, he pressed me to think more deeply about the product I was selling. "Dick," he began, "I have a couple of questions about this type of policy." He said he understood that a whole life insurance policy includes two elements, with part of the cost paying for the actual insurance against risk and the rest deposited into some sort of a "cash-value" reserve, or savings account. I confirmed that he was correct. He then asked, "Can you tell me how much of my premium payment goes toward each of these two purposes?" After a bit of hesitation, I admitted, "I don't know." He continued, "Well then, can you tell me what the rate of return is on this policy? I know what my value of money is, and if you can show me the yield, I can make a decision." After more hesitation, I confessed I didn't know that either. He drove his point home, "Don't you think you should?" In that brief encounter, I realized I knew virtually nothing about the financial structure of a life insurance policy. I assured my challenger that I would seek the answers and bid a hasty retreat from his office. In not too much time I came upon a wise actuary named Homer Adams who offered, "I will teach you how the policy is built, but you will probably leave the insurance business." What I learned from Homer as well as other knowledgeable acquaintances, especially Clint Hendricks, Sonny Nichols, and Don McCormick, and through my own research, shaped my business career and is the basis for this book. My purpose in writing is to empower people to find the correct insurance for their families at the lowest possible cost. This book is not a complicated manual full of technical jargon for aspiring actuaries but rather a common sense roadmap through the life insurance maze for anyone. It is written with readers in the United States in mind, although most of the principles apply elsewhere. After reading this book, you will know more about life insurance than just about any agent who has ever sought your business.

What Is Insurance?

Insurance is a risk-sharing arrangement in which the unexpected losses of a few are borne among the many. Farm community cooperatives are a quaint illustration of the principle by which insurance companies function today. In some farming communities of yesteryear, if one member's barn caught fire and burned down, the neighbors would all pitch in and build a new barn. If one farmer died, others would support the widow and children. Cooperatives became impractical when community bonds weakened and not enough members participated, and eventually insurance companies emerged to fill the vacuum. Insurance companies facilitate risk-sharing by anticipating the likely number of annual loss claims and then charging a per-customer cost called a premium high enough to cover the total predicted losses. The premium charges must be enough for the company to pay for customer loss claims, cover business expenses and still generate a profit. With some forms of insurance, like property, casualty and liability insurance, it's relatively difficult to predict annual losses. Natural disasters such as hurricanes, floods and fires can strike unexpectedly and cause dramatic fluctuations in levels of claims. Since these policies are generally issued for a period of one year, one way companies deal with sudden surges of claims in the wake of catastrophes is to increase their future premium to make up the difference. In some extreme cases, companies may cancel policies or refuse to renew them at their anniversary date.

Despite the uncertainty, casualty insurance claim rates can nevertheless be forecast with rough precision. Yet by contrast, life insurance claim rates can be forecast with virtually absolute certainty. The figures for life insurance are so predictable that in the U.S. no legal reserve life insurance company (one maintaining the minimum financial reserves required by state law) has ever failed to pay a death claim on account of insufficient funds. That is an astounding record for security, but it also suggests very comfortable profit margins in the industry. Public regulation of life insurance has reinforced stability, though ironically insurance regulation has probably benefited the companies more than it has the people themselves. Insurance companies have welcomed regulations preventing them from selling at prices too low to cover policyholder claims, recognizing the threat otherwise of potential crisis in consumer confidence.

Historically in England, the earliest modern life insurance policies were negotiated for one year at a time, and companies based pricing on their own projections. As life insurance took root in the United States, pricing remained varied and inconsistent. Some U.S. companies used outdated statistical projections borrowed from England; others employed their own varying projections. Seeking a basis for more standard pricing, representatives of the industry commissioned an actuary named Sheppard Homans with the task of compiling a uniform death rate table to be used by all insurance companies. Homans was then an employee of the Mutual Life Insurance Company of New York, which was a prominent firm in operation since 1842. His work was published in 1868 as the American Experience Mortality Table (**Exhibit 1**) and remained widely in use until the 1940s. He used data from 1843 to 1858 to calculate how many people on average would die at different ages. This table illustrates that based on his calculations, 7.80 people out of a thousand could be expected to die at age 20, 8.43 at age 30, 9.79 at age 40, 13.78 at age 50 and 26.69 at age 60. Shortly after publication of his findings, Homans felt he had miscalculated his figures slightly, concluding that people would not generally die as young as he had

7

originally thought. Nevertheless, it was not until 50 years later in 1918 that updated life expectancy figures for males were published in a revised American Men's Table, based on statistics from 1900 to 1915. The 1941 Commissioner's Table (**Exhibit 1**), based on data from 1930 to 1940 came next, followed by the 1958 CSO Mortality Table (**Exhibit 1**) and then a 1980 table, using 1970 – 1975 data (**Exhibit 2**). More recently, a 2001 table has been issued (**Exhibit 3**). National Association of Insurance Commissioners (NAIC) regulations called for insurance companies to begin using this new table by 2009. (The NAIC is a non-governmental body issuing model regulations which are largely followed by U.S. state-level insurance regulators. Founded in 1871 to harmonize state rules, the NAIC's membership is composed of state government insurance commissioners.) The tables convey a sense of how the industry forecasts death rates and your life expectancy. Fortunately for us—and the insurance companies—death rates have been steadily going down as people live longer. Despite increased life expectancy generally, the cost of life insurance has essentially remained unchanged through recent decades. Some companies have increased the rates on policies already in effect when the policy provisions have allowed, in part to offset the effects of unusually low interest rates. Although market forces help determine prices, what is constant about life insurance as a risk-sharing arrangement is that those with a statistically greater risk of dying than others pay proportionately more for their insurance.

Why Buy Life Insurance – Personal

Life insurance, when serving its true purpose, is a marvelous product. I had the realization long ago that life insurance was the only bona fide way I knew to create an estate instantly, almost by the stroke of a pen. In essence, the real reason for buying life insurance is to compensate for the economic loss caused by your death. It is that simple. The basic objective is to provide cash to meet the financial obligations you anticipate leaving at your passing, including general living expenses of those who formerly depended on your income, mortgage payments and school tuitions, for example. It's most unfortunate that many insurance companies train their agents to aggressively promote high-priced product variants which include a savings feature extraneous to the real purpose of life insurance. Many insurance people misrepresent life insurance as an instrument for saving for the proverbial rainy day, retirement, education or a myriad other such purposes. Such marketing would entice you into paying much more for your insurance than necessary. Most customers seek life insurance with the simple goal of preparing financially for the death of a major income earner. Rooted in a natural human aversion to death, though, may be an attraction to broader claims for life insurance as a means of providing for the insured's own life rather than merely his death. In earlier times, some men were reluctant to leave behind a wealthy insurance widow, fearing she might just spend the money on a new partner. In reality, though, life insurance tends to have an opposite effect. Statistics show that widows who are well-provided-for tend not to remarry or are more selective when they do.

It's important to understand that one's need for life insurance changes over time, usually according to stages of the life cycle. A child generally has no need to be life-insured. Although the death of a child is an emotional loss, economically it is usually a gain, eliminating the financial burden of supporting the child, including costs for food, clothing and education and perhaps ultimately wedding expenses. Typically, children remain economic burdens until they marry and/ or establish themselves in careers. One exception to the rule that children don't need insurance is the rare circumstance in which family history indicates that poor health may cause the child to risk becoming ineligible for insurance by the time it is needed, if not obtained young. (Passing a physical examination is a requirement for obtaining life insurance, which the chapter on "Underwriting" will discuss.)

Newlywed couples do not need insurance until they themselves have children. Without children the death of either partner does not create a substantial economic loss, except in an unusual circumstance in which the couple has undertaken financial obligations requiring both incomes. The dramatic change in insurance needs comes when the couple begins to have children. The responsibility to care for the new arrivals until they come of age creates a legitimate need for life insurance, although this need itself is not perpetual. Eventually the children will take financial self-responsibility as they grow up, or the parents may save enough money to cover life expenses for the family in the event of the loss of either or both spouses. At such point in the game of life insurance, you win! You no longer need life insurance. Everyone should aim to reach this point. (Nevertheless, there are other situations in which life insurance may still be appropriate, and these will be discussed in subsequent chapters.)

Why Buy Life Insurance – Business

The most common form of business life insurance is group insurance provided by employers as an option for employees. By law as of this writing, the premium on the first $50,000 of individual coverage under an employer-sponsored group life insurance plan is tax deductible and is not reported as employee income for federal tax purposes. The cost of any amount of individual coverage over $50,000 is taxable as a fringe benefit and is reported on a special 1099 form. The cost of group life insurance per-employee is roughly an average based on the ages and risk levels of all of the participants. Special rates and terms for employees in superior health may frequently be provided through what are called group "carve-outs."

A form of life insurance which compensates a company for the loss of important personnel is called "**key-person**" life insurance. This kind of insurance is most important for small to medium-size companies, which can be greatly damaged by the loss of a single valuable person, more so than large companies with broad resources to cushion such losses. Another form of business life insurance is used to fund buy-sell agreements, which allow a business or partnership to buy out a member's interest upon decease. Buy-sell agreements generate the funds needed to pay off the heirs of a deceased member, freeing both the heirs and the remaining members from further unwanted financial entanglement. A final business purpose of life insurance is to provide collateral for banking obligations. Many lending institutions will require a corporate (or personal) borrower to purchase debt insurance sufficient to ensure repayment of the loan obligation.

How Life Insurance Works

Imagine you were going to open a life insurance company that would sell strictly policies with a death benefit of $1,000. You would first need a good estimate of how many people would die at each age. This would be necessary to determine how much to charge for each policy to cover the death claims. If you consulted the 2001 Mortality Table, you would find that 1.72 men out of a thousand could be expected to die at age 40. If your company sold a $1,000 policy to a thousand customers all age 40, you could anticipate that 1.72 people among your customers would die within the year, which would require you to pay $1,720 in claims ($1,000 x 1.72 = $1,720). According to the underlying principle of life insurance, which is to diffuse the burden of losses of the few among the many, the total cost of $1,720 would be divided among the 1,000 participants, leading to a per-member cost of $1.72 per $1,000 of insurance coverage. In this simplified scenario, the number of expected deaths per thousand in the mortality table equals also the dollar cost per thousand. Thus, the mortality table functions essentially as an insurance company rate table. By putting a $ sign in front of the deaths per thousand you obtain a rate per thousand. This is the minimum amount your company should charge for $1,000 of life insurance. In addition to this base figure, you would want to charge enough to cover expenses and make profit. This is the fundamental make-up of "term insurance"—the original form of life insurance. Term refers to how it is sold for limited (often renewable) periods, or "terms." Really, all insurance is term insurance. Some insurance policies add other features such as savings accounts, but even in these policies, the insurance element functions like classic term insurance. Other categories of insurance, such as auto, home owner and professional liability insurance, generally do not add on savings accounts. So why would there be a savings account attached to life insurance? In some cases, there may be a tax deferral advantage. Any amount you pay over and above the amount required to cover the insured risk is retained in a reserve, referred to as the "cash value." Tax on interest earned on the cash value of a life insurance policy is deferred, meaning it does not have to be paid until the policy is surrendered. Even then, the taxable amount is limited to the amount of the surrender value in excess of the premiums that have been paid. The addition of a savings account turns a term insurance policy into a cash-value policy, which may be called "whole life," "universal life," "variable universal life" or some variation thereof.

Our hypothetical company would make a nice profit thus insuring the total population without adding any savings feature to their product. But consider this!......... We know we can expect that 1.72 people out of a thousand will die at age 40. If we could predict which of them specifically will die and exclude them from coverage, what would happen to our profit? The obvious answer is that it would increase dramatically. Can we do it? The answer is a resounding yes! Typically when you apply for life insurance, you do not receive it unconditionally as a random member of the population or some group of 1,000, but instead you must qualify for it by passing financial, physical and moral exams. Note that the life insurance companies rather than the medical societies control the standards for the health exams. Roughly 2-3% of all applicants are rejected, and 4 to 6% are offered coverage only at special higher rates. Thus, 60 to 90 people out of a thousand are denied coverage at standard rates even though only 1.72 out of a thousand will die at age 40. (**Exhibit 4**)

How challenging for insurers is the selection process? If without any prior training you were asked to review the profiles of

1,000 applicants age 40, including their driving record, foreign travel, hazardous activities, medical history, results of a current physical exam, blood and urine tests, and perhaps an electrocardiogram, do you think these would provide you a reasonable means of selecting the 80 individuals with the highest probability of death? Surely an individual who has cancer or heart disease, scuba dives below 40 feet, flies an airplane or has a felony conviction would jump off the page. This ability to predict death based on health and lifestyle is a tremendous advantage combined with the original knowledge that only 1.72 of the total applicants will actually die at this age. Insurance companies and their expert underwriters have evolved a screening process that is so effective that the death rate among first-year policyholders is actually much lower than the rate for the general population, falling closer to one in a million. Precise figures are hard to find, though, because so few die in the first five years of holding a policy that statistical references do not generally even bother to show figures for the first five years. You might almost say you can guarantee immortality by passing an insurance physical each year! It's not so far from the truth. Statistically, it is virtually impossible to die within a year from the time you can pass a life insurance physical. Clearly, insurance companies can make a substantial profit just from selling pure insurance. Sale of the most inexpensive term insurance policies alone is very profitable for the insurance companies.

Pure Insurance

The purest form of life insurance is term insurance, sold by definition for a specified duration, or "term," and renewable typically annually. The yearly cost of term insurance generally rises as one ages, with pricing following closely the mortality table. Prior to the 1970s, most term policies were renewable only till age 70—obviously a disadvantage for those requiring coverage beyond the age of 70. In 1978, United Investors Life introduced the first modern term policy that was annually renewable to age 100. (They provided this new policy with or without an optional savings account.) Annually renewable term insurance policies proliferated, with some carrying guaranteed renewal rates. Others offered an option for "re-entry," with a lower rate for those able to pass a new physical at each policy anniversary date. (Note even with policies that do not have a formal re-entry option, you can achieve the effect of re-entry any time you are able to qualify for new insurance with a cost equal to or lower than the existing contract, whether through the same or a different company.)

Because term pricing is straightforward and not complicated by the addition of an accumulation savings account, it is easy to compare costs between policies. The ease of comparison has encouraged the controversial practice of **policy replacement**, which will be addressed at length in a later chapter. Agents at the grassroots level encouraged people to exchange policies for new ones that the buyers could obtain at lower rates, rewarding the agents also with a NEW commission for selling a NEW policy for each replacement. Insurance companies perceived this essentially fair practice as a significant threat. To curtail replacement of life insurance policies, many companies began aggressively marketing policies offering guaranteed level premiums, to age 65 or for the first five to thirty years the policy was in effect. To calculate pricing for guaranteed level premiums, companies simply add up the annual mortality cost for the length of the guaranteed period, discount the total by an assumed interest rate and then divide by the number of years. The resulting average price is paid per year. The principle is that the customer overpays for the initial few years and then underpays for the remainder. The sales logic behind this practice is that after paying a higher price for a few years, a customer would be less inclined to replace the policy. The major advantage of a level premium term policy for consumers is that the annual cost is guaranteed to not rise above a certain level, even if deteriorating health makes failure of a new physical examination likely. The disadvantage is that those continuing in good health generally pay a higher price for coverage than they would without the guaranteed rates, and those who die in the early years of a policy with a longer level premium effectively overpaid for the coverage.

Since there is no way to eliminate participants who become ill from guaranteed renewable policies, insurance companies must anticipate illness rates when they set initial prices. For instance, if a company insures one-thousand people age 40 who have successfully passed all of the examination requirements, it is highly unlikely that any of those individuals will die in the first year of the policy. The pool of insureds at this stage is virtually pure. Over time, though, some in the group will begin to experience health problems and their chance of dying will increase. If there was some way to continually exclude the unhealthy people, the initial and continuing cost would be lower for the other participants. But a guaranteed renewable policy by definition rules out this possibility. So the only way healthy members generally can take financial advantage of their good fortune is to purchase a new policy, leaving the group they are with and joining a new one. The success of the strategy is dependent on fair and consistent pricing within the insurance industry.

Term replacement has continued to annoy the insurance industry. The NAIC promulgated the Life Insurance and Annuities Replacement Model Regulation in 1998, indirectly curbing the practice. The pretext that certain companies were not charging high enough premiums for policies offering guaranteed rates for longer than ten years was justification for new regulations requiring the companies to hold a portion of the yearly premiums from such policies in a special reserve account for the life of each policy. To compensate for the frozen funds, the companies found it necessary to increase rates. The regulation seeks paternalistically to ensure company solvency but has functioned in effect more as justification for boosting prices of life insurance. Consider this question. If the projected premium for a customer at age 40 were X, but the actual charge were X plus $1.00 and the $1.00 was held in reserve for the duration of the policy, what would you say should happen to the $1.00 at the termination of the policy? By the logic of fair pricing for term insurance, the $1.00 should be returned to the policyowner, if and when the policy is surrendered. Unfortunately, the insurance companies in practice keep such reserves, meaning that consumers pay too much for their policies. A side effect of the higher cost since the year 2000 has been to dampen the replacement of term policies.

Whole Life—The Level Premium System

In contrast to pure insurance, sold for a limited "term," is so-called "permanent insurance," in its most common form of "whole life" boasting a "level premium." Before considering the level premium concept, let your eyes scan the mortality table and look at the death rate from age 0 to age 100. The death rate goes up, so the cost of insurance must unavoidably go up as you grow older. It is an unfortunate reality that there is no legitimate, practical way to entirely escape the increasing costs of life insurance as one ages. The life insurance industry has vainly promised that customers can avoid rising costs by purchasing whole life policies which maintain a level premium to age 100. Misleading advertisements have reinforced this sales pitch. An early typical one by the Institute of Life Insurance equated level premiums with the wonders of space technology, opening: "The level premium system is part of a moon rocket. Right?" This particular ad, shown in **Exhibit 5**, appeared in prominent publications such as *Time*, *Reader's Digest*, and *Sports Illustrated*. In a whole life insurance policy, as illustrated by the semaphore diagram in **Exhibit 6**, a seemingly level premium masks increasing actual costs for insurance. Let's assume that the face amount of this sample whole life policy is $1,000, the premium is $10, and that it was purchased at age 40 and will run to age 100, at which time it ends, or "endows." ("Endowment" is industry jargon for when the policy ends—when the cash value has reached the point of equaling the face amount.) If you have ever purchased a whole life policy or listened to a sales presentation, consider three basic questions. Did the agent lead you to believe that there is a level amount of insurance—in other words, that the company will pay $1,000 upon your death? You would hope the answer is yes because you would not want your beneficiaries to receive less than you had intended. Second, is it your impression that the cost will remain level during the life of this type of contract—that you pay the same regular amount throughout? Certainly, you would not want the cost to change after the policy was in effect. Third, have you heard the claim that with level premium insurance you can save money by buying young? All these three are common beliefs about whole life insurance. Now, if all three proved to not actually be true, how would it affect your confidence in this type of policy? Indeed, in reality all three notions are false. The policies provide neither a level amount of insurance nor level costs, and moreover they do not allow you to save by buying at a younger age. The revelations would be startling to almost anyone. Here's why the three assumptions are false. A whole life policy combines two elements, an increasing cash value plus a decreasing amount of real insurance, with the combined total of the two always equaling an unchanging face amount (**Exhibit 7**). If you die in the first year, when there is no cash value (some companies have first year cash values but most do not), how much will the company pay? The answer is $1,000, the payoff amount indicated in the policy (**Exhibit 8**). If you do not die and wanted to compute your cost per thousand dollars of coverage, you could divide the premium by the coverage amount and multiply by $1,000, which will then provide the cost per thousand. In this illustration, there is $1,000 of insurance and the premium is $10; therefore, the cost per thousand is $10. You now realize that you could have purchased a term insurance policy for much closer to $1.72, but you remember your objective was to have a level cost over a long period of time and so you don't give it further consideration. At some point in time, the cash value will reach $100 (**Exhibit 9**). If you died the moment this happened, how much would the insurance company pay? Again, the answer is $1,000, the amount the policy has always promised to pay. Interestingly, many people think the amount would be $1,100 (the cash value plus the face amount). But they are wrong. In the words of Mort and Albert Gilbert, you would need to "accomplish the contradiction of both dying and living at the same time" to get both the cash value and the face amount —a practical impossibility. In this example, the company pays the $1,000 claim, $100 of which is presumably already your money. But how much of the total must the insurance company pay you out of their funds? The answer is $900. To compute the cost of the insurance to you at this point, you divide the $10 premium payment by the $900 pay-out amount and multiply by $1,000, and the cost per thousand becomes $11.11. What has happened to the cost? It went up! From $10 per thousand to $11.11 per thousand. Amazing! What a clever scheme by the insurance industry to camouflage the increase in the cost of insurance by giving less insurance for the same payment and implying the cost remains level. Consider an analogy. A shopper complains to her grocer about a steep increase in the cost of food. The grocer replies: "Not so. You have been spending the same $100 a week in my store for the last five years." But she points out "Yes, but I used to get ten bags and now only get five bags." Indeed, fewer goods for the same outlay. Let's continue our illustration of the level premium policy. As time passes, the cash value will build up to $500 (**Exhibit 10**). If you die, the company will still pay $1,000, but $500 of the total is your money and $500 is their money. Calculating the cost per thousand of coverage (dividing the premium by the payout and multiplying by $1,000), you'll see that your cost per thousand has increased to $20. You can find an indication of how level premium policies really work if you ever borrow funds from your policy (**Exhibit 11**). The insurance company will include a note with the loan encouraging you to repay the loan as promptly as possible because in the event of death any remaining indebtedness against the contract will be subtracted from the face amount the insurer pays your beneficiaries. The moment you take a $500 loan against a $1,000 policy, you become aware that the death benefit has been reduced to $500. But it does not end there. Insurance companies do not process your loan for free, you must pay interest. Loan interest rates of 5, 6, 7 or even 8% are not uncommon. At a casual glance, such rates may seem reasonable compared, for example, to the typical interest on a credit card. But any interest at all on an insurance loan is too much, when you consider that you are paying the interest for the privilege of borrowing what you believe is really your own money. So, the loan interest is an additional cost on top of a gradually decreasing amount of coverage for your money. So let us return to our three questions. First, do we have a level death benefit? Yes. Do we have a level face amount? Yes. But do we have a level amount of actual insurance? The answer is no. The insurance industry shuffles words, tricking us into thinking the face amount and the death benefit are the same as actual insurance. Next, do we have a level premium? Yes, in the sense that we have a level outlay, but do we have a level cost? Obviously no, because the real cost goes up each year. Finally, do we save any money by buying young? The answer here is also no. The life insurance industry cleverly masks the inescapable reality that the cost of life insurance increases as we age. Buying young would prevent higher costs only for those customers who might happen to develop health problems at an early age. But the math of the mortality tables is inexorable, forcing costs to increase as you get older. Adding cash value in this manner just exacerbates the situation. Unfortunately, the story told by the diagonal lines in **Exhibits 6-11** will not be found in the text of most policies, nor is there a diagonal line across the front of the policy to warn the unwary. Therefore, it is virtually impossible for most buyers to recognize this truth merely by reading the policy. Our closer examination reveals that the level premium system is less of a "moon rocket" than a hoax—one to entice the insurance-buying public to pay too much money for their coverage. The industry is rapacious, callously cheating families who can barely afford even the basic coverage they require let alone bear the burden of paying extra.

Most people make good decisions when provided all the facts. As a buyer, you should now consider whether you were given all the information you needed at the time of your last purchase. If you are an insurance agent, ponder whether you are offering the full truth to your current and prospective clients.

Participating and Non-Participating

Whole life as well as term insurance may be sold in the form of either "participating" or "non-participating" policies. "Participating" policies are sold by mutual life insurance companies that are owned by the policyholders. They offer what is referred to as a dividend— although unlike a stock dividend this payment is not a share of company earnings but essentially a refund of a portion of the policy cost. Participating policies are more typically whole life. The Internal Revenue Service is not fooled by the label "dividend" and treats them as refunds rather than earnings for tax purposes, not requiring life insurance dividends to be reported as taxable income.

Customers pay extra, called a "load," for the dubious privilege of receiving a refund in an amount that is variable and at the discretion of the insurance company. The base premium cost a company must charge to meet the obligations of a whole life insurance policy to age 100 is referred to as the "net level premium," and the amount charged in excess of the net level premium is the load. The company can do what it wants with the load. It can retain it as additional profit or can accumulate it in a pool of funds called the "divisible surplus" for use to pay dividends in future years. Companies are careful to disclose to buyers that dividends are not guaranteed and can be changed at any time at the discretion of the company, but most customers sadly do not recognize the ramifications. When a company declares dividends, it may provide them in cash, in the form of reduced premiums, in additions to policy savings left to accumulate interest, or as payment for additional insurance called "paid-up additions." A fifth dividend variation offers one year's worth of term insurance equal to the policy cash value with the remainder of the dividend amount, if any, applied to one or more of the other options.

Are dividend paying participating policies a good value for the consumer? A life insurance executive quoted by Dave Goodwin in *Best's Review* (December 1973) admitted that the overcharge on participating polices was the best money maker he knew of: "What other way do you know of in any business to get a person's money, offer no goods or service for it, not even a promise to return the money at all, ever—no commitment of any kind, and then, after using it to make money for ourselves for years, to return as much or as little as we want on a schedule we ourselves set?"

Non-participating policies are issued by stock life insurance companies. Because they do not offer dividends, these policies have a smaller load and therefore offer a lower guaranteed annual premium for the same amount of insurance. The attraction of dividend-paying policies is largely illusory and a gamble. Even what dividends are paid benefit only those insured individuals who survive to receive them, and the promised benefit is lost or reduced for those who happen to die soon after buying a policy.

Universal Life Insurance

Universal life (UL) insurance is a more recent innovation, a "new era" product which emerged in the midst of the high interest rates of the mid to late 1970s and early 1980s. As rising interest rates eroded the savings value of existing whole life policies, many policy owners preferred to withdraw or borrow funds from their life insurance and re-invest elsewhere. Loan interest of 6% (which at the time was tax deductible), compared favorably with common earnings of 18% in a money market account. In reaction, many traditional insurance companies abandoned their lucrative but flagging trade in whole life insurance policies in favor of new, flexible-premium, "adjustable" life (universal life) policies.

In contrast to the set payment structure and guaranteed benefits (the "defined benefit plan") of a whole life policy, a universal policy offers a voluntary money purchase option, a sliding benefit based on how much the customer wishes to pay in. In simple terms, a universal life policy is a term insurance contract with the addition of an optional, rather than mandatory savings account. Contracts for the "accumulation" policies feature guaranteed minimum interest rates and guaranteed maximum premium costs. Among other differences from whole life, universal offers 1) transparent disclosures of charges and the cost of insurance, 2) interest and tax-free policy withdrawals up to the cost basis (total premiums paid), and 3) an "Option B" providing a death benefit that includes the cash value rather than just the face amount.

Generally, a universal policy will remain in effect as long as there are sufficient funds within the contract to pay for the monthly term insurance cost. In the framework of this new type of policy, the insurance companies were able to offer much higher (though non-guaranteed) interest rates for the savings component. Many companies systematically sought to persuade customers to replace their whole life policies with universal ones rather than lose customers to competitors. Companies armed their agents with misleading policy illustration software to support the claim that universal life featured a "vanishing premium" opportunity made possible by the higher returns. These illustrations made the premium vanish by projecting unrealistic long term yields without factoring in the potential for interest rates to fall (to a minimum rate allowed by the policy fine print) or for the cost of insurance to increase. The failure of such overly optimistic promises incited numerous class action suits against insurance companies. Although universal life policies are less expensive than traditional whole life, they are still more expensive than simple term insurance.

Another variation of universal life has a "no lapse" feature. As long as the policyholder pays the premiums on a timely basis and does not take out any policy loans, the death benefit is guaranteed until the insured reaches age 120. Because the premiums go toward covering the cost of long-term insurance, the policy accumulates little or no surrender value, and therefore functions in effect like extended term insurance.

Variable Universal Life

Variable universal life (VUL) is a special type of universal life insurance. Like universal life in general, it features a "flexible premium" and is "adjustable," that is, policyholders may contribute as much or as little as they like to a policy's cash value. What's unique about variable universal life is that such payments can be deposited into mini-mutual funds referred to as sub-accounts, as well as into more conventional fixed interest savings-type accounts with yields similar to those in a regular universal life policy. Although the optional equity (stock) component can potentially outperform fixed income, in practice it usually does not. Sales agents tend to emphasize the investment feature more than the value of the life insurance. Agents often promote these policies as a way to buy mutual funds with tax deferred earnings. While it is true that variable products enjoy the same tax deferral as whole life ones, agents usually avoid disclosing that upon cancellation, or "surrender" of a variable life policy, when the tax on the earnings comes due (if there are any earnings at all), the tax is usually substantially higher than it would be on the comparable earnings of an independent mutual fund account. Conventional, standalone mutual funds enjoy special "capital gains" tax rates, which in most circumstances are much lower than standard tax rates (a legal incentive to invest, rationalized as compensation for the risk involved). In contrast, earnings from the sub-account component of a surrendered VUL insurance policy are taxed at regular income rates.

Another problem with these policies is that to be profitable, sub-accounts require management expertise beyond what most buyers or even sellers have. In addition, variable universal life policies tend to be more expensive than regular universal life. One reason is the "mortality charge," which is a monthly fee that increases as a policyholder ages. As a standard feature of all universal life insurance policies, the mortality charge may often be 25% higher in a variable policy than in a non-variable one. In addition to the high mortality charge, variable policies are saddled by an especially numerous array of other fees. Variable life does have one special advantage in that the sub-accounts are considered segregated funds that are immune from seizure by a life insurance company's creditors in the event of corporate financial problems, such as a number of insurance providers have experienced historically, including for example Confederation

Life, Mutual Benefit Life and Executive Life. Most striking among drawbacks, though, is that even the modest potential for greater earnings with a variable universal life insurance policy is usually realized only if the owner surrenders the policy before death. If the owner dies while still holding the policy, the cash value is generally irrelevant because the company will pay only the face amount (unless it's an "Option B" type policy). The incentive to cancel policies before death counters the essential purpose of life insurance, which is death coverage. So in most cases, the policyholder's perpetually elusive quest for greater cash value returns through a variable policy is like the proverbial donkey seeking his carrot. The cash value carrot keeps getting bigger, but the poor donkey never gets any closer to the tasty orange vegetable.

Indexed Universal Life

Hailed as a next-generation product, Indexed Universal Life (IUL) carries less risk than variable universal life while maintaining good growth potential. Like VUL, it features sub-accounts, but those in an IUL policy are not comprised of actual securities. Instead, the IUL sub-accounts provide returns based on the performance of market indexes. The returns typically have a "floor" (minimum) rate of up to 3% and a maximum "cap" of around 12%, which limit volatility for the insured and the provider, respectively. Gains are credited based on the value of the index at the end of each participation period, typically one or two years, and are then locked in so cannot afterward be lost. Most also include a participation rate whereby the insurer gets a portion of any gains, typically anywhere from 25% up. An indexed policy with 6% growth at the end of a twelve-month period with a participation rate of 50% would see an increase in value of 3%. Although less volatile than VUL, with the potential for solid if not as dramatic growth, indexed universal life is a complex product with many moving parts and options that may be confusing to customers and require substantial professional guidance. More importantly, the actual cost of insurance in an IUL policy is still greater ultimately than if you buy term insurance.

Commissions

The public generally knows very little about the commissions agents earn for selling life insurance policies. The insurance industry does publish some market figures, but individual agents are not required and usually prefer not to inform their clients of their compensation for sales. By contrast, buyers of securities (stocks and bonds) are generally better informed of such details through prospectuses or offering circulars, which sellers are required to publish. Insurance companies have long manipulated agent compensation rates to favor sale of preferred products. When I first began selling life insurance close to fifty years ago, the typical commission earned on a term insurance policy was 40% of the first year's premium and 5% of each subsequent premium paid in the second through tenth years. The commission on whole life insurance was 75% of the first year's premium and 10% of premiums in the second through tenth years. At that time, New York State had some unique regulatory limitations; companies operating there could offer their agents commissions of no more than 55% for the first year, but to help make up the difference they offered an expense reimbursement benefit.

Given the typical figures at that time, if I sold a $100,000 term policy with a premium of $200, my commission was $80 ($200 x .40% = $80). If a fellow insurance agent sold a $100,000 whole life policy with a premium of $600, his compensation was $450 ($600 x .75% = $450). Who did better? Both sold $100,000 policies, but one was paid $80 and the other $450, more than five times as much. Today's compensations differ, but the bias in favor of cash-value policies remains. A typical agent's commission on a term insurance policy with guaranteed level rates for periods of five to thirty years is 75% to 95% of the first year premium, usually paid in a single lump sum called "heaped compensation," with no subsequent commissions on annual renewals. Universal life and variable universal life policies typically pay commissions of 100% of the first year payment and renewal commissions of 1 to 2%. Agents are not required to inform you of their compensation up front, but you can request to see a copy of the agent's selling agreement with the insurance company. Details in the selling agreement will make very clear the bias in favor of cash-value policies. In *What's Wrong with Your Life Insurance*, Norman F. Dacey summarizes eloquently the dilemma of the life insurance agent: If you sell term insurance you can't eat, but if you sell cash-value insurance, you can't sleep. The Occidental Life advertisement in **Exhibit 12**

highlights the sharp disparity in compensation.

Low-Load/No Load Life Insurance

Low-load life insurance was a revolutionary innovation,
though unfortunately its availability has waned in recent years. In
its heyday it was one of the most consumer-friendly forms of life
insurance. Banker's Life of Nebraska introduced this new product in
response to the high cost of commissions, which typically consume a
substantial portion of the first year premium. The vast effort required
by life insurance companies to administer commissions is reflected
in corporate structure, with "Commissions" typically one of the three
main company divisions, right alongside "Home Office Administration,
Underwriting Policy Service" and "Marketing Allowance, Advertising,
Sales Management and Distribution." Banker's Life of Nebraska came
upon a workable way to eliminate the agent's commission, benefiting
both the company and customer by substantially increasing policy
performance and additionally providing greater liquidity in the first
years of coverage than a traditional "front-end loaded" policy (with
more heavy initial premium payments). Agents who proffered the
new low-load policies could abandon the commission reimbursement
model, which earned them income only for successful sales. Instead,

they could choose to earn their income through charging a consulting service fee for educating the customer. In this way, agents would make money regardless of whether their clients ultimately decided to buy. Other companies followed the lead of Banker's Life of Nebraska and used their marketing budgets to interest and train agents in selling life insurance under the new arrangements. The insurance community was slow to embrace the new concept, prompting *Consumer Reports* in August 1993 to describe "low-load" life insurance as the best kept secret in the insurance industry (**Exhibit 13**).

Unfortunately, in the context of company mergers and acquisitions, early leaders in the field of low-load insurance, such as Bankers Life and Southland Life, have largely abandoned the innovation. A few scattered low-load life insurance products remain available, but they target special markets which don't match the profile of most buyers. Those in the know long for a resurgence of low-load products for the general public.

Commission rebates are an alternate means of achieving a low-load effect. The rebates in essence share the agent's commission with the customer, but they are illegal as of this writing in all states except Florida and California. Even where legal, tax considerations discourage the practice, since the policy owner is required to report the rebate as taxable income. So commission rebates do not fill the gap left by the retreat of the non-commission low-load policy.

Cost Comparison

Smart shopping for life insurance requires some objective means of comparing the cost of policies. Historically, the insurance industry has emphasized comparisons of cost relative to "living benefit" (that is, benefit during the insured's lifetime). The approach catered to a perceived preference of buyers to avoid thinking about their own mortality. The traditional "net cost" approach to policy comparison measured the difference between the premium paid versus the total (living) benefit, including the cash surrender value at any time plus any projected dividends. The resulting figure often was a (too-good-to-be-true) negative cost to the buyer. Living benefit amounts were typically calculated for periods of 10 or 20 years after policy enrollment or as of the insured's age of 65. Today, the "interest-adjusted cost method" is preferred, providing a more accurate result that takes into account the time value of money. Using this method, cost figures are provided both for living benefit (surrender cost index) and death benefit (net payment cost index). Any measures emphasizing living benefits, however, tend to obfuscate the true cost of life insurance. Facing squarely the reality of the ultimate purpose

49

of a life insurance policy to provide a benefit at death, a "death" cost analysis provides the clearest measure. The simplicity may surprise some. For term policies, just divide the policy premium by the face amount and you obtain the true cost of life insurance per $1,000 of coverage. Essentially the same process will reveal the true cost of cash-value policies, except for minor variations in inputs for cost and death benefit. (Variations include, for example, premium paid via policy loan on whole life or from the cash value in a universal life policy.) Calculating in this simple manner the true cost of life insurance per $1,000 of death benefit provides a reliable and objective standard for comparison of cost for competing life insurance policies.

Replacement

The U.S. Constitution supports the right of citizens to enter into contracts free of excessive interference from government or other third parties. Article 1, Section 10 bars states from passing laws "impairing the obligation of contracts," and the Fifth, Ninth and Fourteenth Amendment protections of personal liberty vouchsafe a broad freedom to enter into private contracts as long as they do not violate laws. In general in the United States, you have the right to open or close a bank account, sign up for or cancel a credit card and buy or sell stock. In addition, you have the right to change banks, credit card companies or brokerage firms, and you may usually do so without giving any prior notification to your former account holder. This seems reasonable and just, and should presumably apply to most personal business transactions. Unfortunately, the life insurance industry has a different mindset and seeks to curtail policy exchange by various means, beginning with attaching pejorative labels. "Exchange," according to a common dictionary definition, is "the act of substituting one thing for another" (*Webster's*). This term seems adequate to describe the process of canceling one life insurance policy and buying a new one. The insurance industry, though, has preferred the term "replacement," with a subtle negative connotation.

Policy replacement became an issue during the Great Depression, following saturation of the market in the 1920s with expensive insurance products. Wise agents offered customers new, more affordable contracts as alternatives to the more expensive policies they currently held. The transactions benefited clients in multiple ways. Clients generally recovered substantial funds, were able to pay off any outstanding policy loans, and found themselves with policies better suited to their families' needs at a lower cost. Such agents were providing a vital service to their customers, but the insurance companies turned a baleful eye. An industry media campaign portrayed policy replacement as a predatory sales practice and source of financial loss to customers. Calvin Coolidge, then director of the New York Life Insurance Company, delivered a famous anti-replacement message on October 6, 1931, which had significant repercussions. Coolidge warned: "Do not let anyone persuade you to alter or switch your policies without the best advice of the companies that issued them.... Beware of the so called 'twister' and 'abstractor' or any agent who offers to save money for you by replacing your policy in another company." In reaction, insurance freelancer Lewis B. Tebbetts sued Mr. Coolidge and the New York Life Insurance Company for misrepresentation and they settled out of court. Coolidge actually sent Tebbetts a personal letter of apology. Nevertheless, the insurance industry continued unabated its crusade to discourage the replacement of older policies, without regard to whether or not replacement was in the best interest of policyholders. The cover of the pamphlet, *Don't Let the Twister Twist You*, shown in **Exhibit 14,** was typical of the campaign against policy replacement.

Preparing for my insurance career, I took a course offered by the Life Underwriter's Training Council (LUTC), where I received an instruction that "any old policy is better than a new one." I also encountered admonishments in the Equitable Life Insurance Society rate book like, "Agents who replace existing policies should be driven out of the business." The book counseled, "Never sell a term policy if it is possible to sell a permanent policy." At the time I began my career, the issue of replacement had abated in the atmosphere of relative national prosperity following World War II. Only a few actuaries and enlightened salesmen were promoting replacement.

But such activity intensified again during the 1960s and early 1970s, this time fueled by a dramatic increase in interest rates and the new product called universal life. Previously, replacement had typically involved substitution of new cash-value policies for old ones, but now term insurance policies were increasingly substituted. As a result of a comprehensive industry campaign to disparage term insurance, agents loyal to whole life were often zealous in their intolerance of those selling term. Verbal exchanges between opposing sides could be heated and colorful. In the effort to buoy up whole life, industry propaganda steered the terms of the debate from the economic merits of the products toward emotionalized and ultimately irrelevant issues of philosophy coupled with character assassination.

State insurance regulators furthered the bias against policy replacement. An Ohio Department of Insurance bulletin from 1981 shown in **Exhibit 15** offers a stern warning to licensed insurers against improper policy replacement. It reflects the common position of state regulators. Note that although the bulletin responds to "a significant number of complaints" against the practice, these are complaints from "other agents" rather than from consumers. The regulatory regime ultimately has less to do with protecting customers from dishonest practices than it does with shielding insurance providers from loss of business.

The bias persists and is reflected in current life insurance applications. In a typical application, there is a section asking the potential customers to list all their other active insurance policies. This question appears innocuous, in the seeming best interest of both parties, perhaps to prevent the purchase of more insurance than the customer can afford or reasonably qualify for. The next question, though, more clearly reveals the industry's motivation to discourage replacement: "If this policy is approved as applied for, will it replace any existing policies?" If the applicant checks "yes," the form probes further, asking, "Which contracts will be replaced, and why will they be replaced?" In the agent's report submitted along with the application, there is a similar question, "Do you have reason to believe that this policy will replace any existing life insurance policies?" If either the applicant or the agent answer "yes" to these questions, they must complete a "Notification of Replacement" (replacement form).

This form is used to fulfill regulatory requirements for notification of the company whose policy is being replaced. In the case of a cash surrender policy, the form will note whether the proceeds will be used to purchase a new cash-value contract. Perhaps to avoid intruding too boldly upon the customer's freedom to contract, NAIC regulations hold agents more accountable than customers for the accuracy of information entered on the forms. Regulations provide that applicants have the right to replace existing policies even after indicating a contrary intention, but that patterns of such action by clients of the same agent will be deemed prima facie evidence of the agent's intent to violate the regulation. In other words, applicants have the right to answer the question "no" and then act otherwise without it constituting misrepresentation, but agents do not. New NAIC model regulations dated March 1, 2007, seek even more detailed disclosures regarding contemplated policy replacements. Insurance regulation through the industry-dominated NAIC clearly discourages the exchange of existing policies for new ones. It's really remarkable how smoothly state insurance regulators further the interests of the large insurance companies at the expense of consumers' rights through adoption of the NAIC guidelines.

Confrontations

Salesman hate to lose clients for many reasons—it's not just the loss of business and money, but also the loss of a relationship, and a client's trust. Ironically, it may be the hardest to lose a client when it's for a good reason. Agents who lose clients through replacement of whole-life insurance with term may resort to personal attacks. I have experienced my share of such confrontations at close hand. After I moved with my family from Houston to my wife's hometown of Chagrin Falls, Ohio in 1970, I was building a thriving practice, adding between two to four new clients a week. As most of the sales involved replacing existing whole life insurance policies with new term insurance coverage, I was quickly becoming the least popular agent in the life insurance community. A few experiences were particularly memorable.

One evening at home I was startled to receive a phone call around 10:30 at night from a hostile New York Life agent who demanded, "What is the wonderful thing you have for Mr. Fisher?" I was informed my new client had told the agent, "If you really want to learn about life insurance, you should talk to Dick Bodwell."

The agent was so upset that he filed a complaint with the Cleveland Association of Life Insurance Agents, and I was called before the Ethics Committee for a hearing. After the association was notified that my client would not give his consent for me to discuss all of his personal insurance matters with the committee, I heard nothing more of the complaint. Around that time I learned another agent was kicked out of the association when he discussed the benefits of term insurance on a radio show, including a comment that agents who sold whole life insurance were either dishonest or stupid. Although the agent's comments were blunt, I was disturbed by the abrupt dismissal and decided to resign from the group myself.

One morning, I was threatened with physical violence by an agent who lost business to me. Through referrals, I had replaced whole life policies for several of his former clients who were physicians at Brentwood Hospital in Warrensville Heights, Ohio. Over the phone, he growled, "If you don't stop taking my clients at Brentwood Hospital, I am going to beat you up." I offered to meet him at the end of my driveway and gave him my address. Fortunately (for him), he didn't show up.

An experience I enjoy recounting was when a local attorney invited me to his office to debate the merits of whole life versus term with a friend who sold him insurance. I reluctantly agreed but told him that it would not be pretty. When we met I introduced myself and asked the agent who he represented. He proudly responded, "New York Life" and asked me the same question. I responded firmly that I represented Mr. Griffiths (the customer). After a pause (I don't think the agent knew quite how to respond), I asked if he wanted to go first, but he invited me to. So I drew a familiar semaphore diagram, such as found in **Exhibit 6**, and asked him if this represented a whole life insurance policy. When he responded, "Yes," I told Mr. Griffiths that I had nothing else to say and left. The next day, Mr. Griffiths called me and said he was ready to sign an application for term insurance.

I was able to avoid future confrontations by warning new clients that replacement of their insurance would very likely upset the former agent. I suggested they be prepared to communicate a simple statement such as, "I appreciate what you have done for me in the past, but I am making changes to my life insurance program, the matter is confidential and I am not at liberty to discuss it." This short statement has proven to be an effective bar to further complaint, as the other agent does not want to look unreasonable by pressing further. The replaced agent typically sees no choice but to gracefully withdraw. I had an occasion to laugh when a client practiced the same advice on me, and I protested it was no fair. (The client explained his son had gone into the life insurance business, and he wanted his son to have the business.)

Choosing a Company

If you decide to purchase a life insurance policy, you will need

to choose a company. Life insurance companies tend to offer similar

products, but your choice of company can be important, especially

if you may be a likely candidate for a more expensive risk category

as a result of health, age, or lifestyle. Most companies sell products

catering to one or two niche markets, and you may find a particular

company is the best match. You should also look at life insurance

company ratings which measure financial strength, particularly if you

are interested in a policy with some form of cash value. The cash

value may only be as good as your company's solvency. (Beware,

though, there are multiple rating systems with different lettering

schemes to indicate rank, so be sure you are comparing apples to

apples.) Norman Dacey noted that during the Great Depression

approximately 14% of operating life insurance companies went into

receivership by 1936. They failed on account not of their insurance

business but rather their banking function. Financial strength of a

company is a factor in choosing insurance, but you can be reassured

that no U.S. life insurance company maintaining the minimum

financial reserves required by law has ever failed to pay a death claim. Even the smallest company that maintains adequate reserves for legal operation will pay your beneficiaries in the event of your death. Even when a company goes bankrupt, states guarantee that beneficiaries get paid, up to any limits of mandatory payment set by state law. In 1973 Equity Funding Corporation of America (EFCA) went into bankruptcy following litigation for securities fraud. In 1983 Baldwin United filed for bankruptcy but the company paid all outstanding death claims.

Underwriting

In order to purchase a new policy or replace an existing policy, you will need to pass the insurance company's underwriting requirements. Underwriting is the process whereby a company prices and issues a life insurance policy according to your relative risk of dying, as reflected in your assignment to a particular "rate class." At one time there were only two rate classes, male and female. Statistically, women live longer than men. As a result, their life insurance rates are lower. Other factors being comparable, a woman at age 40 will pay about the same premium as a male age 37. (Some female clients are pleased to learn that their "insurance age" is younger than their natural age!) Most companies calculate insurance age as of the year of your birthday that is nearest to the date of policy enrollment rather than your latest birthday previous to enrollment. That means your insurance age and your rates will go up one year if you enroll more than six months after your birthday. According to the mortality tables, your risk of dying, or death rate, is level for a full year, but the prevalent practice of the life insurance actuaries is to spike the cost of coverage for anyone purchasing a policy less than six months before the next birthday. To avoid this uptick in cost, you can either purchase soon after a birthday or find one of the rate companies that calculates age based on the latest birthday (though the advantage of the latter option may be outweighed if the company's product otherwise has a higher cost).

A further major rate class distinction has evolved for tobacco versus non-tobacco consumers, with separate rates for both males and females. Non-tobacco users may be further subdivided into super preferred, preferred, standard plus, and standard rates. Tobacco users are subdivided into preferred tobacco and standard tobacco. Some companies will offer preferred non tobacco rates to individuals who smoke a limited number of cigars per year, and standard non-tobacco rates even to those who chew or regularly smoke cigars, smoke a pipe, or use marijuana.

When you submit an application for life insurance, it is essential that you provide accurate information. Misrepresentation of any material fact is one of the (rare) reasons a company may deny payment of a claim. (Another is suicide within the first two policy years.) Remember that insurance companies have access to medical databases with your history, including pharmacy records, so inaccuracies and omissions in your application are likely to be detected. As part of the application process, your insurance company will ask your physician for information regarding your medical history, and you will normally need to undergo a physical examination, including a resting electrocardiogram (EKG) and analysis of blood and urine samples. Tests may be administered by paramedic services onsite at your home or place of business. To increase your chance of the most favorable possible test results, recommended preparation includes engaging in some form of aerobic exercise for three of the seven days prior to your exam and minimizing consumption of alcohol and high-sugar and high-fat foods during the same period. Inquire about the weight limit for the various rate classes based on you height, and try to lose a few pounds if it may qualify you for a better rate class with lower premiums. "Grooming the applicant" in this way, as it is known in the industry, may result in cost savings that may range from 15% to 50%. It is well worth the effort.

Applicants will often say to me, "I will apply just after I get checked out by my personal physician." Don't do it! Unless you have a condition requiring treatment, avoid doctors for the short time until your new policy is in effect. Otherwise, you may risk increased costs or even a complete denial of insurance if you learn of a new medical problem just before you buy a policy. Your goal is to pass the insurance underwriting requirement, not to stay out of the Army! The insurance company will typically pay for your blood test that will be performed by an independent practitioner, and the results can be shared afterward with your regular doctor.

How Much Is Enough?

If you determine you need life insurance, the next question you ask yourself is how much and for how long? Enough is the amount that will support your loved ones or fulfill your other purposes in the event of your decease. Do keep in mind there is a subjective element, as the amount needed will vary depending on your lifestyle and personal goals relative to what you can afford. Remember also that your insurance agent has a vested interest in encouraging you to buy more. Years ago, I heard a speaker at a life insurance sales seminar quip, "I have never known a beneficiary to complain that the check was too big." While that may be true, don't be afraid to think independently and conclude if you need less insurance than your insurance agent may be suggesting with the best intentions. How long you need insurance can be something of a guessing game. "If you will tell me when you are going to die, I can tell you what to buy" is a tongue-in-cheek but true answer. Despite the inherent uncertainty, you can build stable plans that account for likely eventualities and need. For analysis of your needs, the best sources of assistance are estate planning attorneys and fee-only financial planners who do not sell products. They are trained to properly guide you and help answer the questions of how much and how long.

Waiver of Premium

Some insurance policies will offer an optional waiver of premium rider. The rider is an add-on that will cover your cost of insurance or premium in the event you become disabled. There is typically a waiting period following disability, sometimes called an elimination period, of three to six months before the rider benefit will take effect. Waiver of premium riders vary in how broadly they define disability, and it's important to recognize the differences. The best riders will define disability the most broadly, for example as a condition in which you are unable to perform the duties of your regular occupation. Average riders will define disability more narrowly as the inability to perform duties that are reasonably suited to your education, training or experience. The narrowest will define disability as the inability to do anything for wage or profit. A rider with such a limited definition of disability would not waive your premium unless you were unfit for even the lowest paying jobs. Waiver of premium riders may ultimately benefit the insurance companies more than they benefit you as the customer, since the rider is guaranteeing that the insurance company will continue to receive its payments on the policy. Before buying waiver of premium, I recommend you buy waiver of rent, groceries, clothes, and essentials. It may sound odd, but this is what a stand-alone disability income policy will provide—a monthly income you can use for any purpose. It will cost less than the waiver premium rider offered by most companies.

Accidental Death

Accidental death insurance is sometimes called double indemnity. Its purpose is to provide your beneficiary with funds in the event you die as a result of an accident. It may appear inexpensive compared to the cost of policies that cover both sickness and accident, but it is still overpriced relative to the risk. It is commonly sold at airports or as part of a group insurance benefit. To understand why accidental death insurance is not a good bargain, ask yourself this question. Would the manner in which you die, whether by accident or from natural causes, make any real difference in the amount of money your beneficiaries will need for support in your absence? The answer is almost always no! Thus we recommend you buy the amount of life insurance your beneficiaries will need and do not gamble on how you are going to die.

How to Pay Your Premium

Most companies offer four payment period options: annually, semiannually, quarterly and monthly. If you pay other than annually, you will face a surcharge. A typical semiannual payment is 52% of the annual cost. At first glance 4% may not seem like a bad surcharge. If your annual premium is $100, paying $52 two times a years does not seem bad. But let's take a closer look at the math. For the privilege of holding $48 for six months longer than you would if you paid the annual cost all at once, you have paid a "borrowing" fee of $4, which divided by $48 is an interest rate of slightly more than 8% for six months, or an annual interest rate of over 16%! If you were to choose a quarterly payment for your insurance, a typical quarterly cost is 26% of the annual premium. A typical monthly payment cost is 8.5% of the annual premium. These also amount to borrowing at a fairly high rate of interest. Until companies are required to better disclose the true cost of financing, you should pay annually if possible since it is the lowest cost option.

Policy Beneficiary

A beneficiary is any individual or legal entity identified in a life insurance policy to receive benefits upon the decease of the insured. If a life insurance policy has no named beneficiary, its proceeds will become part of the deceased's estate and subject to creditors and probate. The simple act of naming a beneficiary can avoid all this. Policies typically identify both "primary" and "contingent" beneficiaries. The contingent beneficiary will receive the policy proceeds in the event the primary beneficiary predeceases the insured. The most common beneficiaries are spouses, children, and other family members. If you wish minor children to benefit from your insurance policy, special treatment is advisable. If you name minor children directly as either primary or contingent beneficiaries, the probate court may manage their affairs until they reach the age of majority, when they would receive a lump sum portion of the proceeds. This creates inconvenience for the children's guardians who must go to the judge and justify each expense in order to care for the children. The common solution is to execute a revocable trust and name the trust as the primary or contingent beneficiary of the life insurance policy.

Your minor children will be the beneficiaries of the trust to be managed by a trustee whom you select, according to your direction as expressed in the trust document.

Policy Ownership

Most life insurance policies are owned by the insured. Ownership of the policy carries various rights, including the privilege to name or change beneficiaries. Proceeds from such insurance policies carry the benefit of not being subject to U.S. federal income tax, but, treated as part of the deceased's estate, they may be subject to federal and state estate tax. You can avoid estate tax, however, by establishing an irrevocable life insurance trust (ILIT) and grant ownership of the policy to the trust. Creating the trust involves naming the beneficiaries and the grantor (usually the insured) and making a gift to the trust in an amount sufficient to pay the premium of the insurance policy. At death, the proceeds are paid to the trust and therefore are not considered part of the insured's estate.

Less commonly, life insurance policies may also be owned by employers or business partners. An employer may purchase a policy on the life of an employee, perhaps to compensate for loss of valuable services. Such policies typically require the employer to advise the employee of the amount. The proceeds from the policy will generally be tax free if the employer obtains a signed disclosure form that the insurance company will keep on record.

When You No Longer Need Insurance

There may come a point when you realize you no longer need life insurance. Typically, you would surrender the policy and recover any value including unearned prepaid premiums. If the insurance you are terminating is a cash-value policy, you will need to report any gain as taxable earned income. (Your insurer will provide you with a 1035-R document with the exact amount.) Unfortunately, a converse benefit is not available. If you receive less upon surrendering than you paid in, you are unable to deduct any losses from your taxable income. The only way to salvage the loss is to exchange your unneeded policy for a new annuity. Any future gains in the annuity would be tax free until the earnings of the annuity equaled the loss carryover. A capable advisor can assist you with this type of transaction.

Another option is to sell your policy to a third party through a viatical or life settlement. A viatical settlement is the sale of a policy on an individual who has become terminally or chronically ill and is not expected to live more than two years. "Viatical" comes from the Latin word "Viaticum" used in Catholicism for the sacrament of Communion offered to the dying. A life settlement is a similar transaction except that the insured who sells is not necessarily chronically or terminally ill, though is usually over sixty-five years of age. Both are sold for more than the cash surrender value (more than the seller could obtain through surrender) but less than the net death benefit (thus promising the buyer a profit). The buyer of the contract becomes the policy owner and beneficiary and is responsible for any future premium payments.

These settlements can be the best option in appropriate circumstances, benefiting both parties, though ownership of an economic interest in the death of a stranger may be distasteful to some. Because of potential for abuse, and because they may cut into traditional insurance profits, they are tightly regulated. They affect general pricing of insurance which is often what is called "lapse-supported." Insurers can provide prices that are lower than needed to cover the actual cost of insurance (the shared risk) because a predictably large number of policies which will lapse before the death of the insured, through failure of the payment of premiums. A high rate of lapse means insurance companies pay out less in death claims. Viatical and life settlements upset this balance by providing an incentive to keep in force many unneeded policies that might otherwise lapse. When insurers have to pay out more death benefits as a result, they will earn less or must raise prices. Your advisor can help you determine if a viatical or life settlement is right for you and facilitate the transaction in keeping with the regulatory requirements.

Market Trends

Although whole life or permanent insurance long dominated the U.S. market, the economic shock of the Great Depression spurred interest in term insurance. The looming specter of economic failure forced some life insurance providers to see their cash-value cash cow was ill, and some turned from an emphasis on whole life to term insurance. Groundbreaking publications educating the public on the true nature of life insurance included the 1936 book, *Life Insurance: A Legalized Racket* by Mort Gilbert and E. Albert Gilbert, and the 1958 book by actuary K.P. Chartier, *Your Pocketbook Is Leaking*. Both urged buyers to avoid cash-value policies and buy term. Even with increasing public awareness, term insurance did not surge in popularity until the 1980s when there were three primary forces at work. First, very high interest rates and inflation spurred demand for all forms of insurance, as consumers sought to protect their families' finances. Second, the newly emerging financial planning profession encouraged the growth of term insurance in particular. As financial planners studied life insurance, they became enlightened about its pricing and increasingly recommended term insurance to their clients. Third, life insurance agents were increasingly working as independent contractors rather than insurance company hires. Agents were thus no longer captive agents forced to sell strictly a single employer's proprietary products, and they were no longer as discouraged from selling term insurance. The resulting increased demand for term insurance coupled with longer life expectancy led to lower mortality rates and a price war. Companies continually lowered rates. Additionally, companies began experimenting with new alternatives to term, such as universal life insurance, which while not as lucrative as whole life, was more profitable for the sellers than pure term insurance. In the race to be competitive, life insurance companies expanded into the investment business while continuing to promote cash-value polices, emphasizing their largely chimerical tax benefits.

In recent years, many companies have faced a new challenge. Lower interest rates since 2007 have stressed companies with large numbers of older fixed income insurance policies in force that guarantee higher returns than current rates can support. Many life insurance executives may not be sleeping well at night and are eagerly hoping for higher interest rates. Whatever the cause, several companies have simply stopped insuring or have resorted to desperate measures including drastic price increases. Jackson National Life suspended the issue of new individual life insurance policies on August 2012. Allstate sold off Lincoln Benefit Life (LBL) without notice to its officers in August 2015 to the Resolution Life Group (UK), a liquidator which specializes in in-force policies and does not sell any new life insurance policies. Genworth in 2016 notified its sales field it will no longer be offering individual life insurance policies. Transamerica and Voya (formerly ING Security Life) increased the cost of insurance on existing non-guaranteed accumulation universal life policies, some by as much as 44%. Such price increases are risky; if customers bolt to cheaper competitors, these companies could be left with nothing but the uninsurable risks. The potential for companies that emphasize cash-value products to fail in the current market is another reason most buyers should put their money prudently elsewhere and buy term.

Conclusion

The sum of all this is fairly short and simple. As Herb Page, the golf coach at Kent State University, told me that he advises his young players, "Buy term life insurance and make money while you sleep." What great advice. (I would just add to that, pay your premiums annually to avoid interest.) Buying term life insurance is the least expensive way to replace the economic loss created by one's death. Adding any form of savings account just increases the cost of the insurance. When buying your life insurance, hold your agent to the responsibility of securing for you the appropriate amount of coverage at the lowest possible cost. In addition, ask him to review your coverage annually and let you know if lower rates become available. Over a lifetime, you will save a fortune.

Suggested Reading

Chartier, K. P., *Your Pocketbook Is Leaking*. Dallas: Chartier. 1958.

Dacey, Norman F., *What's Wrong with Your Life Insurance*. New York: Macmillan. 1989.

Gilbert, Mort, and E. Albert Gilbert, *Life Insurance: A Legalized Racket*. Philadelphia: Marlowe. 1936.

Katt, Peter C., *The Life Insurance Fiasco: How to Avoid It*. West Bloomfield, Mich.: Dolphin. 1992.

Reynolds, G. Scott, *The Mortality Merchants: The Legalized Racket of Life Insurance and What You Can Do about It*. New York: David McKay. 1968.

Sudzius, Linas, *What Most Life Insurance Agents Won't Tell You*. Nashville: Wax Family Printing. 2012.

EXHIBITS

MORTALITY TABLES

Age	American Experience (1843-1858)		Commissioners 1958 Standard Ordinary (1950-1954)		Individual Annuity Table for 1971—Male (1960-1967)		Individual Annuity Table for 1971—Female (1960-1967)		United States Total Population (1969-1971)	
	Deaths Per 1,000	Expectation of Life (Years)	Deaths Per 1,000	Expectation of Life (Years)	Deaths Per 1,000	Expectation of Life (Years)	Deaths Per 1,000	Expectation of Life (Years)	Deaths Per 1,000	Expectation of Life (Years)
0	154.70	41.45	7.08	68.30	—	—	—	—	20.02	70.75
1	63.49	47.94	1.76	67.78	—	—	—	—	1.25	71.19
2	35.50	50.16	1.52	66.90	—	—	—	—	.86	70.26
3	23.91	50.98	1.46	66.00	—	—	—	—	.69	69.34
4	17.70	51.22	1.40	65.10	—	—	—	—	.57	68.39
5	13.60	51.13	1.35	64.19	.46	71.69	.23	76.99	.51	67.43
6	11.37	50.83	1.30	63.27	.42	70.73	.19	76.01	.46	66.46
7	9.75	50.41	1.26	62.35	.40	69.75	.16	75.02	.43	65.49
8	8.63	49.90	1.23	61.43	.39	68.78	.14	74.03	.39	64.52
9	7.90	49.33	1.21	60.51	.39	67.81	.13	73.04	.34	63.54
10	7.49	48.72	1.21	59.58	.39	66.84	.13	72.05	.31	62.57
11	7.52	48.08	1.23	58.65	.40	65.86	.14	71.06	.30	61.58
12	7.54	47.45	1.26	57.72	.41	64.89	.16	70.07	.35	60.60
13	7.57	46.80	1.32	56.80	.41	63.91	.17	69.08	.46	59.62
14	7.60	46.16	1.39	55.87	.42	62.94	.18	68.10	.63	58.65
15	7.63	45.50	1.46	54.95	.43	61.97	.19	67.11	.82	57.69
16	7.66	44.85	1.54	54.03	.44	60.99	.21	66.12	1.01	56.73
17	7.69	44.19	1.62	53.11	.46	60.02	.22	65.13	1.17	55.79
18	7.73	43.53	1.69	52.19	.47	59.05	.23	64.15	1.28	54.86
19	7.77	42.87	1.74	51.28	.49	58.07	.25	63.16	1.34	53.93
20	7.80	42.20	1.79	50.37	.50	57.10	.26	62.18	1.40	53.00
21	7.86	41.53	1.83	49.46	.52	56.13	.28	61.19	1.47	52.07
22	7.91	40.85	1.86	48.55	.54	55.16	.29	60.21	1.52	51.15
23	7.96	40.17	1.89	47.64	.57	54.19	.31	59.23	1.53	50.22
24	8.01	39.49	1.91	46.73	.59	53.22	.33	58.25	1.51	49.30
25	8.06	38.81	1.93	45.82	.62	52.25	.35	57.27	1.47	48.37
26	8.13	38.12	1.96	44.90	.65	51.28	.37	56.29	1.43	47.44
27	8.20	37.43	1.99	43.99	.68	50.32	.39	55.31	1.42	46.51
28	8.26	36.73	2.03	43.08	.72	49.35	.41	54.33	1.44	45.58
29	8.34	36.03	2.08	42.16	.76	48.39	.44	53.35	1.49	44.64
30	8.43	35.33	2.13	41.25	.81	47.42	.47	52.37	1.55	43.71
31	8.51	34.63	2.19	40.34	.86	46.46	.50	51.40	1.63	42.77
32	8.61	33.92	2.25	39.43	.92	45.50	.53	50.42	1.72	41.84
33	8.72	33.21	2.32	38.51	.98	44.54	.57	49.45	1.83	40.92
34	8.83	32.50	2.40	37.60	1.05	43.58	.61	48.48	1.95	39.99
35	8.95	31.78	2.51	36.69	1.12	42.63	.65	47.51	2.09	39.07
36	9.09	31.07	2.64	35.78	1.20	41.68	.70	46.54	2.25	38.15
37	9.23	30.35	2.80	34.88	1.30	40.73	.75	45.57	2.44	37.23
38	9.41	29.62	3.01	33.97	1.40	39.78	.81	44.60	2.66	36.32
39	9.59	28.90	3.25	33.07	1.51	38.83	.87	43.64	2.90	35.42
40	9.79	28.18	3.53	32.18	1.63	37.89	.94	42.68	3.14	34.52
41	10.01	27.45	3.84	31.29	1.79	36.95	1.01	41.72	3.41	33.63
42	10.25	26.72	4.17	30.41	2.00	36.02	1.09	40.76	3.70	32.74
43	10.52	26.00	4.53	29.54	2.26	35.09	1.19	39.80	4.04	31.86
44	10.83	25.27	4.92	28.67	2.57	34.17	1.29	38.85	4.43	30.99
45	11.16	24.54	5.35	27.81	2.92	33.25	1.40	37.90	4.84	30.12
46	11.56	23.81	5.83	26.95	3.32	32.35	1.52	36.95	5.28	29.27
47	12.00	23.08	6.36	26.11	3.75	31.46	1.65	36.01	5.74	28.42
48	12.51	22.36	6.95	25.27	4.23	30.57	1.80	35.06	6.24	27.58
49	13.11	21.63	7.60	24.45	4.74	29.70	1.97	34.13	6.78	26.75
50	13.78	20.91	8.32	23.63	5.29	28.84	2.15	33.19	7.38	25.93
51	14.54	20.20	9.11	22.82	5.86	27.99	2.37	32.26	8.04	25.12
52	15.39	19.49	9.96	22.03	6.46	27.15	2.64	31.34	8.76	24.32
53	16.33	18.79	10.89	21.25	7.09	26.33	2.97	30.42	9.57	23.53
54	17.40	18.09	11.90	20.47	7.74	25.51	3.35	29.51	10.43	22.75
55	18.57	17.40	13.00	19.71	8.42	24.71	3.79	28.61	11.36	21.99
56	19.89	16.72	14.21	18.97	9.12	23.91	4.28	27.71	12.36	21.23

Age	American Experience (1843-1858)		Commissioners 1958 Standard Ordinary (1950-1954)		Individual Annuity Table for 1971—Male (1960-1967)		Individual Annuity Table for 1971—Female (1960-1967)		United States Total Population (1969-1971)	
	Deaths Per 1,000	Expectation of Life (Years)	Deaths Per 1,000	Expectation of Life (Years)	Deaths Per 1,000	Expectation of Life (Years)	Deaths Per 1,000	Expectation of Life (Years)	Deaths Per 1,000	Expectation of Life (Years)
57	21.34	16.05	15.54	18.23	9.85	23.13	4.83	26.83	13.41	20.49
58	22.94	15.39	17.00	17.51	10.61	22.35	5.41	25.96	14.52	19.76
59	24.72	14.74	18.59	16.81	11.41	21.59	6.02	25.10	15.70	19.05
60	26.69	14.10	20.34	16.12	12.25	20.83	6.63	24.25	16.95	18.34
61	28.88	13.47	22.24	15.44	13.13	20.06	7.22	23.41	18.29	17.65
62	31.29	12.86	24.31	14.78	14.07	19.34	7.77	22.57	19.74	16.97
63	33.94	12.26	26.57	14.14	15.08	18.61	8.29	21.74	21.33	16.30
64	36.87	11.67	29.04	13.51	16.19	17.89	8.78	20.92	23.06	15.65
65	40.13	11.10	31.75	12.90	17.41	17.17	9.29	20.10	24.95	15.00
66	43.71	10.54	34.74	12.31	18.77	16.47	9.89	19.29	26.99	14.38
67	47.65	10.00	38.04	11.73	20.29	15.77	10.62	18.47	29.18	13.76
68	52.00	9.47	41.68	11.17	21.99	15.09	11.54	17.67	31.52	13.16
69	56.76	8.97	45.61	10.64	23.89	14.42	12.66	16.87	34.00	12.57
70	61.99	8.48	49.79	10.12	26.00	13.76	14.03	16.08	36.61	12.00
71	67.67	8.00	54.15	9.63	28.34	13.11	15.65	15.30	39.43	11.43
72	73.73	7.55	58.65	9.15	30.93	12.48	17.55	14.53	42.66	10.88
73	80.18	7.11	63.26	8.69	33.80	11.86	19.74	13.79	46.44	10.34
74	87.03	6.68	68.12	8.24	36.98	11.26	22.26	13.05	50.75	9.82
75	94.37	6.27	73.37	7.81	40.49	10.67	25.12	12.34	55.52	9.32
76	102.31	5.88	79.18	7.39	44.39	10.10	28.37	11.64	60.60	8.84
77	111.06	5.49	85.70	6.98	48.72	9.55	32.05	10.97	65.96	8.38
78	120.83	5.11	93.06	6.59	53.50	9.01	36.23	10.32	71.53	7.93
79	131.73	4.74	101.19	6.21	58.79	8.50	40.98	9.68	77.41	7.51
80	144.47	4.39	109.98	5.85	64.60	7.99	46.39	9.08	83.94	7.10
81	158.60	4.05	119.35	5.51	70.90	7.51	52.51	8.49	91.22	6.70
82	174.30	3.71	129.17	5.19	77.67	7.05	59.41	7.94	98.92	6.32
83	191.56	3.39	139.38	4.89	84.94	6.60	67.16	7.41	106.95	5.96
84	211.36	3.08	150.01	4.60	92.87	6.16	75.90	6.90	115.48	5.62
85	235.55	2.77	161.14	4.32	101.89	5.74	85.77	6.43	125.61	5.28
86	265.68	2.47	172.82	4.06	111.65	5.34	96.90	5.99	137.48	4.97
87	303.02	2.18	185.13	3.80	123.05	4.95	109.34	5.57	149.79	4.68
88	346.69	1.91	198.25	3.55	136.12	4.57	122.98	5.20	161.58	4.42
89	395.86	1.66	212.46	3.31	151.07	4.21	137.51	4.86	172.92	4.18
90	454.55	1.42	228.14	3.06	168.04	3.87	152.47	4.55	185.02	3.94
91	532.47	1.19	245.77	2.82	187.15	3.55	167.37	4.28	198.86	3.73
92	634.26	.98	265.93	2.58	208.46	3.26	181.78	4.04	213.63	3.53
93	734.18	.80	289.30	2.33	231.69	2.98	195.39	3.83	228.70	3.35
94	857.14	.64	316.66	2.07	257.15	2.73	208.07	3.63	243.36	3.19
95	1,000.00	.50	351.24	1.80	283.84	2.50	219.90	3.46	257.45	3.06
96			400.56	1.51	311.57	2.30	231.10	3.29	269.59	2.95
97			488.42	1.18	340.21	2.11	242.21	3.13	280.24	2.85
98			668.15	.83	369.77	1.94	253.82	2.97	289.77	2.76
99			1,000.00	.50	400.19	1.79	266.45	2.81	298.69	2.69
100					431.41	1.65	280.54	2.65	306.96	2.62
101					463.31	1.53	296.45	2.49	314.61	2.56
102					495.76	1.41	314.54	2.33	321.67	2.51
103					528.60	1.31	335.12	2.17	328.17	2.46
104					561.69	1.21	358.54	2.01	334.14	2.41
105					594.88	1.13	385.12	1.85	339.60	2.37
106					628.02	1.05	415.24	1.70	344.60	2.34
107					660.95	.98	449.27	1.55	349.17	2.30
108					693.50	.92	487.65	1.41	353.33	2.27
109					725.52	.86	530.79	1.27	357.12	2.24

Note: Mortality rates contained in the 1958 Commissioners Standard Ordinary Table were obtained from experience of 1950-1954, but contain an added element designed to generate life insurance reserves of a conservative nature in keeping with the long-term guarantees inherent in life insurance contracts. Premiums for life insurance policies, on the other hand, are based on assumptions that include expected mortality experience.

Mortality rates for the 1971 Annuity Tables are, again, conservative as related to the actual experience upon which they are based.

MORTALITY TABLES

Age	Commissioners 1980 Standard Ordinary (1970-1975) Male Deaths Per 1,000	Male Expectation of Life (Years)	Female Deaths Per 1,000	Female Expectation of Life (Years)	1983 Individual Annuity Table (1971-1976)* Male Deaths Per 1,000	Male Expectation of Life (Years)	Female Deaths Per 1,000	Female Expectation of Life (Years)	United States Population (1969-1971) Deaths Per 1,000	Expectation of Life (Years)
0	4.18	70.83	2.89	75.83	—	—	—	—	20.02	70.75
1	1.07	70.13	.87	75.04	—	—	—	—	1.25	71.19
2	.99	69.20	.81	74.11	—	—	—	—	.86	70.28
3	.98	68.27	.79	73.17	—	—	—	—	.69	69.34
4	.95	67.34	.77	72.23	—	—	—	—	.57	68.39
5	.90	66.40	.76	71.28	.38	74.10	.19	79.36	.51	67.43
6	.86	65.46	.73	70.34	.35	73.12	.16	78.37	.46	66.46
7	.80	64.52	.72	69.39	.33	72.15	.13	77.39	.43	65.49
8	.76	63.57	.70	68.44	.35	71.17	.13	76.40	.39	64.52
9	.74	62.62	.69	67.48	.37	70.20	.14	75.41	.34	63.54
10	.73	61.66	.68	66.53	.38	69.22	.14	74.42	.31	62.57
11	.77	60.71	.69	65.58	.39	68.25	.15	73.43	.30	61.58
12	.85	59.75	.72	64.62	.41	67.28	.16	72.44	.35	60.60
13	.99	58.80	.75	63.67	.42	66.30	.17	71.45	.46	59.62
14	1.15	57.86	.80	62.71	.43	65.33	.18	70.46	.63	58.65
15	1.33	56.93	.85	61.76	.44	64.36	.19	69.47	.82	57.69
16	1.51	56.00	.90	60.82	.45	63.39	.20	68.49	1.01	56.73
17	1.67	55.09	.95	59.87	.46	62.42	.21	67.50	1.17	55.79
18	1.78	54.18	.98	58.93	.47	61.44	.23	66.51	1.28	54.86
19	1.86	53.27	1.02	57.98	.49	60.47	.24	65.53	1.34	53.93
20	1.90	52.37	1.05	57.04	.51	59.50	.26	64.55	1.40	53.00
21	1.91	51.47	1.07	56.10	.53	58.53	.28	63.56	1.47	52.07
22	1.89	50.57	1.09	55.16	.55	57.56	.29	62.58	1.52	51.15
23	1.86	49.66	1.11	54.22	.57	56.59	.31	61.60	1.53	50.22
24	1.82	48.75	1.14	53.28	.60	55.63	.33	60.62	1.51	49.30
25	1.77	47.84	1.16	52.34	.62	54.66	.35	59.64	1.47	48.37
26	1.73	46.93	1.19	51.40	.65	53.69	.37	58.66	1.43	47.44
27	1.71	46.01	1.22	50.46	.68	52.73	.39	57.68	1.42	46.51
28	1.70	45.09	1.26	49.52	.70	51.76	.41	56.70	1.44	45.58
29	1.71	44.16	1.30	48.59	.73	50.80	.42	55.72	1.49	44.64
30	1.73	43.24	1.35	47.65	.76	49.83	.44	54.75	1.55	43.71
31	1.78	42.31	1.40	46.71	.79	48.87	.46	53.77	1.63	42.77
32	1.83	41.38	1.45	45.78	.81	47.91	.48	52.80	1.72	41.84
33	1.91	40.46	1.50	44.84	.84	46.95	.50	51.82	1.83	40.92
34	2.00	39.54	1.58	43.91	.88	45.99	.52	50.85	1.95	39.99
35	2.11	38.61	1.65	42.98	.92	45.03	.55	49.87	2.09	39.07
36	2.24	37.69	1.76	42.05	.97	44.07	.57	48.90	2.25	38.15
37	2.40	36.78	1.89	41.12	1.03	43.11	.61	47.93	2.44	37.23
38	2.58	35.87	2.04	40.20	1.11	42.15	.65	46.96	2.66	36.32
39	2.79	34.96	2.22	39.28	1.22	41.20	.69	45.99	2.90	35.42
40	3.02	34.05	2.42	38.36	1.34	40.25	.74	45.02	3.14	34.52
41	3.29	33.16	2.64	37.46	1.49	39.30	.80	44.05	3.41	33.63
42	3.56	32.26	2.87	36.55	1.67	38.36	.87	43.09	3.70	32.74
43	3.87	31.38	3.09	35.66	1.89	37.43	.94	42.12	4.04	31.86
44	4.19	30.50	3.32	34.77	2.13	36.50	1.03	41.16	4.43	30.99
45	4.55	29.62	3.56	33.88	2.40	35.57	1.12	40.20	4.84	30.12
46	4.92	28.76	3.80	33.00	2.69	34.66	1.23	39.25	5.28	29.27
47	5.32	27.90	4.05	32.12	3.01	33.75	1.36	38.30	5.74	28.42
48	5.74	27.04	4.33	31.25	3.34	32.85	1.50	37.35	6.24	27.58
49	6.21	26.20	4.63	30.39	3.71	31.96	1.66	36.40	6.78	26.75
50	6.71	25.36	4.96	29.53	4.06	31.07	1.83	35.46	7.38	25.93
51	7.30	24.52	5.31	28.67	4.43	30.20	2.02	34.53	8.04	25.12
52	7.96	23.70	5.70	27.82	4.81	29.33	2.22	33.59	8.76	24.32
53	8.71	22.89	6.15	26.98	5.20	28.47	2.43	32.67	9.57	23.53
54	9.56	22.08	6.61	26.14	5.59	27.62	2.65	31.75	10.43	22.75
55	10.47	21.29	7.09	25.31	5.99	26.77	2.89	30.83	11.36	21.99
56	11.46	20.51	7.57	24.49	6.41	25.93	3.15	29.92	12.36	21.23
57	12.49	19.74	8.03	23.67	6.84	25.09	3.43	29.01	13.41	20.49
58	13.59	18.99	8.47	22.86	7.29	24.26	3.74	28.11	14.52	19.76
59	14.77	18.24	8.94	22.05	7.78	23.44	4.08	27.21	15.70	19.05

EXHIBIT 2B

| | Commissioners 1980 Standard Ordinary (1970-1975) | | | | 1983 Individual Annuity Table (1971-1976)* | | | | United States Population (1969-1971) | |
| | Male | | Female | | Male | | Female | | | |
Age	Deaths Per 1,000	Expectation of Life (Years)	Deaths Per 1,000	Expectation of Life (Years)	Deaths Per 1,000	Expectation of Life (Years)	Deaths Per 1,000	Expectation of Life (Years)	Deaths Per 1,000	Expectation of Life (Years)
60	16.08	17.51	9.47	21.25	8.34	22.62	4.47	26.32	18.95	18.34
61	17.54	16.79	10.13	20.44	8.98	21.80	4.91	25.44	18.29	17.65
62	19.19	16.08	10.96	19.65	9.74	20.99	5.41	24.56	19.74	16.97
63	21.06	15.38	12.02	18.86	10.63	20.20	5.99	23.69	21.33	16.30
64	23.14	14.70	13.25	18.08	11.66	19.41	6.63	22.83	23.06	15.65
65	25.42	14.04	14.59	17.32	12.85	18.63	7.34	21.98	24.95	15.00
66	27.85	13.39	16.00	16.57	14.20	17.87	8.09	21.14	26.99	14.38
67	30.44	12.76	17.43	15.83	15.72	17.12	8.89	20.31	29.18	13.76
68	33.19	12.14	18.84	15.10	17.41	16.38	9.73	19.49	31.52	13.16
69	36.17	11.54	20.36	14.38	19.30	15.66	10.65	18.67	34.00	12.57
70	39.51	10.96	22.11	13.67	21.37	14.96	11.70	17.87	36.61	12.00
71	43.30	10.39	24.23	12.97	23.65	14.28	12.91	17.07	39.43	11.43
72	47.65	9.84	26.87	12.28	26.13	13.61	14.32	16.29	42.66	10.88
73	52.64	9.30	30.11	11.60	28.84	12.96	15.98	15.52	46.44	10.34
74	58.19	8.79	33.93	10.95	31.79	12.33	17.91	14.76	50.75	9.82
75	64.19	8.31	38.24	10.32	35.05	11.72	20.13	14.02	55.52	9.32
76	70.53	7.84	42.97	9.71	38.63	11.13	22.65	13.30	60.60	8.84
77	77.12	7.40	48.04	9.12	42.59	10.56	25.51	12.60	65.96	8.38
78	83.90	6.97	53.45	8.55	46.95	10.00	28.72	11.91	71.53	7.93
79	91.05	6.57	59.35	8.01	51.76	9.47	32.33	11.25	77.41	7.51
80	98.84	6.18	65.99	7.48	57.03	8.96	36.40	10.61	83.94	7.10
81	107.48	5.80	73.60	6.98	62.79	8.47	40.98	9.99	91.22	6.70
82	117.25	5.44	82.40	6.49	69.08	8.01	46.12	9.40	98.92	6.32
83	128.26	5.09	92.53	6.03	75.91	7.57	51.89	8.83	106.95	5.96
84	140.25	4.77	103.81	5.59	83.23	7.15	58.34	8.28	115.48	5.62
85	152.95	4.46	116.10	5.18	90.99	6.75	65.52	7.77	125.61	5.28
86	166.09	4.18	129.29	4.80	99.12	6.37	73.49	7.28	137.48	4.97
87	179.55	3.91	143.32	4.43	107.56	6.02	82.32	6.81	149.79	4.68
88	193.27	3.66	158.18	4.09	116.32	5.69	92.02	6.38	161.58	4.42
89	207.29	3.41	173.94	3.77	125.39	5.37	102.49	5.98	172.92	4.18
90	221.77	3.18	190.75	3.45	134.89	5.07	113.61	5.60	185.02	3.94
91	236.98	2.94	208.87	3.15	144.87	4.78	125.23	5.26	198.88	3.73
92	253.45	2.70	228.81	2.85	155.43	4.50	137.22	4.94	213.63	3.53
93	272.11	2.44	251.51	2.55	166.63	4.24	149.46	4.64	228.70	3.35
94	295.90	2.17	279.31	2.24	178.54	3.99	161.83	4.37	243.38	3.19
95	329.96	1.87	317.32	1.91	191.21	3.75	174.23	4.12	257.45	3.06
96	384.55	1.54	375.74	1.56	204.72	3.51	186.54	3.88	269.59	2.95
97	480.20	1.20	474.97	1.21	219.12	3.29	198.65	3.65	280.24	2.85
98	657.98	.84	655.85	.84	234.74	3.07	211.10	3.44	289.77	2.76
99	1,000.00	.50	1,000.00	.50	251.89	2.86	224.45	3.22	298.69	2.69
100					270.91	2.66	239.22	3.01	306.96	2.62
101					292.11	2.46	255.95	2.80	314.61	2.56
102					315.83	2.26	275.20	2.59	321.67	2.51
103					342.38	2.08	297.50	2.38	328.17	2.46
104					372.09	1.90	323.39	2.18	334.14	2.41
105					405.28	1.73	353.41	1.98	339.60	2.37
106					442.28	1.57	388.11	1.79	344.60	2.34
107					483.41	1.41	428.02	1.60	349.17	2.30
108					528.99	1.27	473.69	1.43	353.33	2.27
109					579.35	1.13	525.66	1.26	357.12	2.24
110					634.81	1.01	584.46	1.11		
111					695.70	.89	650.65	.97		
112					762.34	.78	724.75	.83		
113					835.06	.70	807.32	.71		
114					914.17	.67	898.89	.60		
115					1,000.00	.50	1,000.00	.50		

Note: Mortality rates contained in the 1980 Commissioners Standard Ordinary Table were obtained from experience of 1970-1975, but contain an added element designed to generate life insurance reserves of a conservative nature in keeping with the long-term guarantees inherent in life insurance contracts. Premiums for life insurance policies, on the other hand, are based on assumptions that include expected mortality experience.

Mortality rates for the 1983 Individual Annuity Tables are, again, conservative as related to the actual and projected experience upon which they are based.

*Projected to 1983.

EXHIBIT 3A

COMMISSIONERS 2001 STANDARD ORDINARY MORTALITY TABLE				
MALE AND FEMALE				
AGE LAST BIRTHDAY				
AGE LAST BIRTHDAY	MALE 1000qx	MALE LIFE EXPECTATION	FEMALE 1000qx	FEMALE LIFE EXPECTATION
0	0.72	75.67	0.42	79.87
1	0.46	74.73	0.31	78.90
2	0.33	73.76	0.23	77.93
3	0.24	72.79	0.20	76.95
4	0.21	71.81	0.19	75.96
5	0.22	70.82	0.18	74.98
6	0.22	69.84	0.19	73.99
7	0.22	68.85	0.21	73.00
8	0.22	67.87	0.21	72.02
9	0.23	66.88	0.21	71.03
10	0.24	65.90	0.22	70.05
11	0.28	64.91	0.25	69.06
12	0.34	63.93	0.27	68.08
13	0.40	62.95	0.31	67.10
14	0.52	61.98	0.34	66.12
15	0.66	61.01	0.36	65.14
16	0.78	60.05	0.39	64.17
17	0.89	59.10	0.41	63.19
18	0.95	58.15	0.44	62.22
19	0.98	57.21	0.46	61.25
20	1.00	56.26	0.47	60.27
21	1.01	55.32	0.49	59.30
22	1.02	54.37	0.50	58.33
23	1.04	53.43	0.51	57.36
24	1.06	52.48	0.53	56.39
25	1.09	51.54	0.55	55.42
26	1.14	50.60	0.58	54.45
27	1.17	49.65	0.61	53.48
28	1.16	48.71	0.64	52.51
29	1.15	47.77	0.67	51.55
30	1.14	46.82	0.70	50.58
31	1.13	45.88	0.75	49.62
32	1.14	44.93	0.79	48.65
33	1.16	43.98	0.85	47.69
34	1.19	43.03	0.92	46.73
35	1.24	42.08	1.00	45.78
36	1.31	41.14	1.07	44.82
37	1.39	40.19	1.14	43.87
38	1.49	39.25	1.20	42.92
39	1.59	38.30	1.26	41.97
40	1.72	37.36	1.34	41.03
41	1.87	36.43	1.43	40.08
42	2.05	35.50	1.53	39.14
43	2.27	34.57	1.65	38.20
44	2.52	33.65	1.79	37.26

COMMISSIONERS 2001 STANDARD ORDINARY MORTALITY TABLE				
MALE AND FEMALE				
AGE LAST BIRTHDAY				
AGE LAST BIRTHDAY	MALE 1000qx	MALE LIFE EXPECTATION	FEMALE 1000qx	FEMALE LIFE EXPECTATION
45	2.77	32.73	1.96	36.33
46	3.03	31.82	2.16	35.40
47	3.25	30.92	2.38	34.48
48	3.42	30.02	2.64	33.56
49	3.64	29.13	2.93	32.65
50	3.91	28.23	3.24	31.74
51	4.26	27.34	3.60	30.85
52	4.70	26.46	3.99	29.96
53	5.21	25.58	4.41	29.08
54	5.83	24.72	4.86	28.21
55	6.52	23.86	5.36	27.34
56	7.26	23.02	5.91	26.49
57	7.95	22.19	6.49	25.65
58	8.63	21.37	7.09	24.82
59	9.42	20.55	7.70	23.99
60	10.40	19.75	8.34	23.18
61	11.59	18.96	9.03	22.37
62	12.98	18.18	9.76	21.58
63	14.47	17.42	10.55	20.79
64	16.04	16.67	11.40	20.01
65	17.65	15.94	12.33	19.24
66	19.27	15.23	13.35	18.48
67	20.96	14.53	14.48	17.73
68	22.74	13.84	15.71	16.99
69	24.69	13.16	17.06	16.27
70	26.94	12.50	18.63	15.55
71	29.71	11.84	20.38	14.84
72	32.94	11.20	22.29	14.15
73	36.32	10.59	24.39	13.48
74	39.96	9.99	26.68	12.81
75	43.95	9.40	29.20	12.16
76	48.44	8.83	31.95	11.53
77	53.67	8.28	34.97	10.91
78	59.72	7.75	38.28	10.30
79	66.48	7.25	41.92	9.72
80	74.02	6.76	46.43	9.14
81	82.20	6.30	51.96	8.59
82	90.82	5.87	57.80	8.06
83	100.22	5.45	63.94	7.55
84	110.69	5.06	70.74	7.07
85	122.36	4.69	77.59	6.60
86	135.17	4.34	85.68	6.16
87	148.99	4.02	95.69	5.74
88	163.00	3.73	106.25	5.34
89	179.03	3.45	116.68	4.96

EXHIBIT 3C

AGE LAST BIRTHDAY	MALE 1000qx	MALE LIFE EXPECTATION	FEMALE 1000qx	FEMALE LIFE EXPECTATION
	COMMISSIONERS 2001 STANDARD ORDINARY MORTALITY TABLE MALE AND FEMALE AGE LAST BIRTHDAY			
90	194.28	3.20	124.22	4.64
91	209.27	2.98	131.53	4.29
92	224.94	2.76	143.72	3.94
93	241.46	2.56	160.21	3.61
94	258.86	2.38	180.90	3.29
95	276.12	2.21	203.48	3.02
96	292.95	2.06	225.69	2.79
97	310.86	1.91	240.07	2.61
98	329.95	1.77	247.79	2.43
99	350.32	1.64	263.98	2.23
100	369.76	1.53	285.02	2.03
101	386.96	1.42	307.89	1.84
102	405.25	1.32	333.06	1.66
103	424.70	1.23	360.71	1.49
104	445.35	1.13	390.86	1.33
105	467.29	1.04	422.72	1.19
106	490.57	0.95	455.33	1.05
107	515.28	0.86	488.48	0.93
108	541.49	0.78	522.20	0.82
109	569.27	0.70	557.04	0.72
110	598.70	0.62	591.96	0.63
111	629.88	0.55	625.62	0.56
112	662.87	0.47	657.77	0.48
113	697.78	0.40	690.79	0.42
114	734.68	0.34	732.06	0.34
115	773.66	0.27	771.35	0.28
116	814.78	0.21	812.36	0.22
117	858.15	0.16	855.90	0.16
118	903.81	0.10	896.58	0.11
119	951.67	0.05	939.06	0.06
120	1000.00		1000.00	

EXHIBIT 4

SELECTION OF RISKS

The great majority of Americans who apply for life insurance are able to get it. About 98% of the applications for ordinary life insurance in the United States are accepted by the life companies, according to the latest in a series of surveys.

Only 2% of ordinary life applications are not acceptable. More than three-fourths of these applicants have serious health impairments, while the remainder are declined because of other factors, including extremely hazardous jobs.

Life companies have been successful over the years in solving the problems presented by two conflicting underwriting objectives. The selection procedures must provide the benefit of life insurance protection to the greatest possible number of people. Yet, in fairness to all policyholders, life insurance companies must take into account individual differences among applicants, such as age, sex, family health background, medical history, occupation and avocation.

With the applicant's written consent, statements about health or risk activities can be checked with the Medical Information Bureau, an association of member life insurance companies founded by medical directors to alert underwriters to inaccuracies, omissions and willful attempts at fraud. The life insurance company may also ask the family physician for additional details about an applicant's health, with the applicant's permission.

Several developments have contributed to the high rate of acceptance of applicants. Extra-risk life insurance policies, with higher premiums to compensate for poor health or hazardous occupations, have made insurance available to many who could not otherwise obtain it. And advances in medicine, job safety and public health have led to more liberal underwriting of policies, enabling many persons to buy insurance at standard rates who would formerly have had to pay higher premiums because of their health or occupations.

Ordinary Life Insurance
Applications in the United States

	1976		1980	
	Number of Policies	Amount	Number of Policies	Amount
ISSUED AND PAID FOR				
Standard	84%	79%	84%	80%
Extra-Risk	5	5	4	4
Total	89	84	88	84
NOT TAKEN BY APPLICANT				
Standard	7	10	8	12
Extra-Risk	1	3	2	2
Total	8	13	10	14
DECLINED BY COMPANY	3	3	2	2
TOTAL	100%	100%	100%	100%

Source: American Council of Life Insurance.

EXHIBIT 5

The level premium system is part of a moon rocket.

Right?

If that definition seems a little off course, it's because we're trying to make a point.

And the point is, too many people know too little about life insurance.

Which is too bad. Because that can cause a family to have too little life insurance. Or not enough of the right kind.

And after all, life insurance

isn't that hard to understand. Take the level premium system, for instance. The level premium is simply one way to pay for life insurance. And here's the way it works.

Since life gets shorter as people grow older, you might expect a life insurance premium to increase year by year. However, the companies have figured out a way for you to spread your payments over the years at a level price.

This lets you put a fixed price on your permanent life insurance —and, incidentally, build cash value into your policy.

Want to know more? We can help.

We're not in the business of selling life insurance. We're

here to help you do a better job of buying it. By giving you the kind of information you need to talk to an agent with a little more confidence than you may have right now.

The fact is, we have a 64-page booklet called *Understanding Your Life Insurance*. The booklet is free. And it's filled with the simple ideas behind complicated-sounding terms like level premium system.

So why not write to us and ask for a copy. We'll mail it to you, fast.

Institute of Life Insurance
277 Park Avenue, N.Y., N.Y. 10017
Central source of information about life insurance.

NUMBER FOUR

This message will appear in the September 14 issue of Time, the September 21 issue of Sports Illustrated and the October issue of Reader's Digest. It is part of a continuing series appearing throughout 1970 and the early months of 1971.

EXHIBITS 6 - 11

EX 6

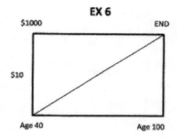

EX 7

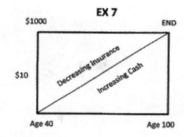

EX 8

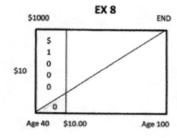

EX 9

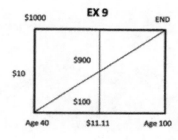

EX 10

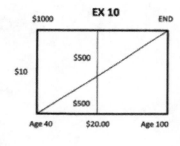

EX 11

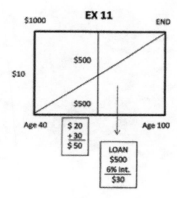

EXHIBIT 12

A broker of ours just brought us a group case.

If it had been strictly group term, his commission this year would have been $463.

It wasn't though. It was Group/Ordinary Life and he earned a first year commission of quite a bit more.

$10,599.

write your name and address here and mail to Occidental Center, Los Angeles 90054

Occidental Life
of California
A Transamerica Company

EXHIBIT 13

LOW-LOAD POLICIES

THE BEST-KEPT SECRET IN INSURANCE

In the last few years, a new breed of universal-life policy has emerged. Called a low-load policy, it imposes significantly lower expense charges on policyholders. You'll find several such policies at the top of the Ratings. Unfortunately, some insurers would rather you not know about these policies, even though they may offer them.

Low-load policies sold by Ameritas, John Alden, USAA Life, Southland, and Peoples Security/Commonwealth Life are a much better value than other universal-life policies in the early years, when most buyers are likely to keep their policies. They also offer good value in the later years for those few policyholders who keep their coverage in force that long.

As we explain in the accompanying report, all universal-life policies subtract expense charges from a policyholder's accumulation fund used to pay sales commissions and marketing expenses. In a standard universal-life policy, those charges can easily approach 100 to 125 percent of the first-year premium. They then taper off in later years.

No agents, low commissions

The insurance agent who sells you a standard universal-life policy typically earns 50 percent of your first-year premium. By contrast, sales commissions and marketing expenses for low-load products amount to no more than 15 to 20 percent of the first-year premium, because there's generally no agent involved. Low-load policies are sold by telephone and through fee-based financial planners (the kind that charge an overall fee but don't receive commissions on the products they recommend).

No policy, however, is totally without charges of one sort or another. Whether they buy low-load or standard universal life, all policyholders must pay the mortality charges for their insurance coverage, as well as some administrative and other expenses. But low-load policies manage to keep those costs significantly lower. Also in their favor, they often impose no, or very low, surrender charges on policyholders who eventually drop their coverage.

A low-load policy is also easier to buy. USAA Life, which has been selling life insurance by phone since the mid-1970s, says the average telephone sale takes about eight or nine minutes to complete.

Fee For Service, in Tampa, Fla., represents a number of low-load companies. It gives free quotes over the phone; the number is 800-874-5662. For a fee of $250, the service will take applications for policies and arrange for the medical examinations the low-load insurers require. If you want advice on what kind of policy to buy, Fee For Service will refer you to one of 750 fee-based financial planners around the country. Fee-based planners typically charge $100 to $150 an hour for their services.

Buying insurance over the phone, however, requires that you know a good deal about the product beforehand. Our reporter called Fee For Service; USAA Life; and Veritas, part of Ameritas, a company that sells one of the top-rated universal-life policies in our survey. She found that the telephone service representatives could provide little information in response to the kind of specific questions an insurance buyer might ask. When she asked a representative of Fee For Service how universal-life policies worked, the representative wouldn't explain but said she'd be happy to send a brochure.

Like the agents who try to sell insurance across your kitchen table, the telephone sellers tended to gloss over the risks of their policies. A representative of Veritas told our reporter that someday she wouldn't have to pay premiums anymore. "The policy will pay for itself out of the cash values," he said. What he didn't mention were the conditions under which those disappearing premiums might reappear.

Reluctant sellers

Predictably, much of the insurance industry is hostile to low-load policies, fearing that if the policies ever catch on in a big way, they will destroy the agent system as it now exists. For similar reasons the few insurance companies that have added low-load policies to their product lines seem to want to keep them secret.

One insurer that submitted a new low-load policy for our study later asked us not to rate it. A former employee of that insurer told us the company had been visited by representatives of an agents' group, who argued that low-load products were not in the best interests of the insurance industry. The company's low-load policy is still not on the market.

Two companies whose low-load offerings rank highly refused to send us their policies; we obtained the information on them through other means. Even Ameritas had to think twice about sharing its low-load policy with us. We also asked Ameritas to submit its traditional universal-life policy to see how the two compared, but Ameritas refused. Such a comparison, apparently, was too touchy a subject for the company's agents.

It's a shame that insurance companies aren't more eager to sell these policies. Low-load policies may not be in the best interest of agents, but they are in the best interest of consumers.

He doesn't tell you that every insurance commissioner has expressed time and again condemnation of the very plan he advocates.

He doesn't tell you that the **United States Chamber of Commerce** has distributed literally millions of leaflets, warning the business man of this country against the loss that almost invariably follows when old insurance is changed for new.

He doesn't tell you that many **Better Business Bureaus** in the United States have, time and again, classed the so-called twister with the crook and the swindler.

Call His Bluff

Tell such a man that you want to submit his proposition to the insurance commissioner's department, or to the company writing the old policy, for expert advice. No matter what reasons he gives you why that wouldn't be the thing to do, no matter how plausible they may sound, you have called his bluff and you can say to him:

"Take off that mask. I know you. You are a twister, but you'll twist no dollars out of me."

FORM 529-1

AMERICAN NATIONAL

Insurance Company

Galveston, Texas

DISTRICT OFFICE

The Twister

[*twisting* The illegal practice of persuading a life insurance policyholder, through misrepresentation, half-truths and incomplete comparisons, to drop or surrender his present policy in one company and buy new insurance in another company.]

Unfortunately almost every business, no matter how carefully conducted it may be, has on its fringe a little group of pirates, or to use a modern term, chiselers—men who make it their business to tear down what others have built up in order to secure a few dollars for themselves in the process.

Life insurance is no exception to this rule.

Despite everything the insurance companies, organized groups of life insurance men, Better Business Bureaus, and insurance departments have been able to do in running this insurance-racketeer into jail, like the sneak thief, he is hard to detect.

Be on your guard against him! Don't let the twister make you his victim!

How to Recognize a Twister

Beware of the man who wants you to lapse a policy, take out the cash surrender value, and buy a new policy in a different company.

Beware of the man who urges you not to consult with the agent or with the company writing the policy you are asked to drop.

Beware of the man who urges you to make the change without taking time for investigation.

Beware of the man who will not leave with you, Above His Signature, his complete proposal to drop insurance in one company and take it in another.

Beware of the man who is one breath criticizes the practices of life insurance companies and in the next breath asks you to buy a life insurance policy.

Beware of the man who seeks to make you dissatisfied with your present insurance program.

Don't try to out-argue him. You can't argue with a white-collar bandit, any more than you can argue with a loaded revolver.

A Tissue of Falsehood

The twister doesn't tell you of the advantages of retaining a life insurance policy which you have owned for some years. Your old policy may contain—undoubtedly does contain—features which cannot be duplicated in the new policy he urges you to buy.

He doesn't tell you that during the early years, a part of the money you pay on the new policy will go toward his commission, the cost of putting the business on the books, making the examinations, issuing the policy—expenses you have already paid on the old policy.

He doesn't tell you that if your old policy is a limited payment or endowment form that in a few, years it will be paid, whereas his policy probably calls for payments as long as you live.

He doesn't tell you, if you have a loan, upon which you are paying 6 per cent interest, that the company is crediting YOU with 3 or 3½ per cent on your reserve.

He doesn't tell you that the cash values on the policy he asks you to buy will be much less advantageous to you than the cash values on the policy he urges you to drop.

EXHIBIT 15

JAMES A. RHODES
Governor

STATE OF OHIO

DEPARTMENT OF INSURANCE

2100 STELLA COURT
COLUMBUS 43215

ROBERT L. RATCHFORD, JR.
Director of Insurance

TO: All Insurance Companies licensed to sell life insurance in the State of Ohio

FROM: Robert L. Ratchford, Jr., Superintendent of Insurance

SUBJECT: Life Insurance Replacement

DATE: May 15, 1981

The Ohio Department of Insurance has received a significant number of complaints from insurance agents who allege that other agents have violated the Life Insurance Replacement Rule 3901-1-36 Ohio Adm. Code. This Bulletin will clarify the purpose, and describe the Department's role, in enforcing that rule.

The rule was promulgated, in conjunction with the Life Insurance Solicitation Rule 3901-1-33 Ohio Adm. Code, to assure that policyholders or prospective policyholders are presented with adequate information to make an informed decision concerning the purchase or replacement of life insurance.

The Department will investigate allegations that an insurer and or agent has intentionally avoided the rule by failing to provide a policyholder with the required forms and other information. In such cases, the policyholder cannot make a truly informed decision. The other insurer and agent involved in the transaction should have the means to verify the accuracy of the information presented to the policyholder; or to present the policyholder with additional information to consider before deciding which policy to purchase.

If all of the required forms and information are presented to the policyholder and the other insurer, the rule should be self-enforcing. The insurers and agents involved in the transaction should be able to make certain that the policyholder fully understands the advantages or disadvantages of competing insurance policies. If, however, an insurer can demonstrate that another insurer or individual agent has consistently misrepresented the terms and benefits of the competing policies, and that the nature of such misrepresentations makes it impossible for the rule to be self-enforcing, the Department will investigate those allegations and take appropriate action pursuant to Sections 3901.19 to 3901.22 inclusive of the Ohio Revised Code.

Every life insurer shall transmit a copy of this bulletin to its field representatives.

Made in the USA
Columbia, SC
05 January 2024